IRISH

HAMILTON HARTY
HIS LIFE AND MUSIC

Sir Hamilton Harty in 1935

HAMILTON HARTY
HIS LIFE AND MUSIC

Edited by David Greer

Blackstaff Press

Published by Blackstaff Press Limited, 255A Upper Newtownards Road, Belfast BT4 3JF.

Designed by Liam Miller

ISBN 0 85640 131 5

Printed in Northern Ireland by Belfast Litho Printers Ltd.

CONTENTS

ILLUSTRATIONS

PREFACE

It is a pleasure to acknowledge the help given so willingly and by so many in the preparation of this book. Much of the information in the biographical chapters is based on the recollections of people in Ireland, and in particular those of Hillsborough. Many musicians, too, have helped by supplying or verifying items of information, and the readiness and enthusiasm with which they have done so is testimony to the affection and respect with which Sir Hamilton Harty is remembered among them.

Thanks are due to the Arts Council of Northern Ireland and the Institute of Irish Studies at Queen's University for grants towards the publication of this book; to the Librarian of Queen's University; and to the following for permission to quote extracts from works in which they hold the rights: Boosey & Hawkes Music Publishers Ltd, Breitkopf & Härtel (London) Ltd, Chappell & Co Ltd, Elkin & Co Ltd, Stainer & Bell Ltd, Universal Edition (London) Ltd, Mr Bernard Shore, Alfred A. Knopf Inc.

The friendly advice and help of Miss Olive Baguley has been an unfailing source of encouragement to the editor and his fellow-authors.

The Queen's University   David Greer
Belfast
September 1978

I HILLSBOROUGH YEARS

John Barry

It has been said (probably by someone who never had to put it to the test) that the best recipe for a happy family is a combination of plain living and high thinking. The idea seems to have originated as an effort to explain why so many famous men have been the sons of country rectories. However this may be, and avoiding optimistic generalization, the adage certainly could have been applied with singular appropriateness to life in the Organist's House in Hillsborough towards the end of the 19th century. The background of the establishment was highly exceptional and requires elaboration.[1]

In 1611 an English soldier-turned-settler named Moyses Hill acquired 5,204 acres of forest and bog in County Down. It belonged to the old Irish chieftain Bryan McCrory Magennes and was centred on a hamlet called Cromlyn with Magennes' fortification on rising ground nearby — about twelve miles south of Belfast. Moyses and his son Peter made this the starting point for a piece of dynasty-building which was to prove to be a spectacular success. Within two hundred years their property had grown to staggering dimensions, the family was rich beyond calculation, and the mud huts of Cromlyn had become Hillsborough, the privileged capital of an estate which was regarded as one of the most astonishing phenomena of the Plantation of Ulster.

In addition to all this it just so happened that at the very time when Georgian taste in architecture was at its height the head of the

---

1. For a detailed history of the village of Harty's birth see John Barry, *Hillsborough* (Belfast, 1962). The principal sources for this chapter are the parish records, the Downshire estate papers (Public Record Office, Belfast), and an incomplete and unpublished Memoir written by Harty towards the end of his life. The Memoir is written in ink on 28 sheets of ruled letter-paper (one side only) and breaks off shortly after his move to London. Much other information in this chapter is based on conversations over many years with the old people of Hillsborough, and with the late Miss Alice Harty.

1

family was a man of outstanding refinement and spirituality. He was Wills Hill, first Marquis of Downshire (1718-93), and with all the money in the world he set about reconstructing Hillsborough with the object of making a place and an environment which would be as full of beauty as an accomplished and cultured landlord could make it. Among the many things which he left to posterity was a church of such architectural and artistic merit that it is now recognised as an irreplaceable part of the national heritage. In the west gallery he had a large organ installed by the incomparable John Snetzler. He brought a certain Michael Thompson, Doctor of Musick, from London to play it. And he established what appears to have been the first stipendiary parish church choir in Ireland.

Thus the pattern of patronage was set. For the next hundred years and more the church's music in Hillsborough was the special care of the Downshires. They selected Thompson's successors and it could be assumed that the Hillsborough organists would be men of worth, since otherwise the Downshires would not have brought them, and paid them, and provided them with an official residence. Maybe the money was not lavish, for it is a common human foible that very rich people often have the curious notion that just because they do not need to count their money, those in their employment do not need to have much money to count. This was the 'plain living' aspect of the organist's existence. But the compensation lay in the cultural environment and all that went with it. In this there was at least the possibility of exercising one's aptitudes for 'high thinking'. The man who was organist in Hillsborough enjoyed a peculiar degree of leisure with security of tenure within the shadow of the Big House, and he had the undoubted benefits of status in the village community due to his possession of an *entrée* to the Castle. Indeed this was a sort of gilt-edged passport not only within the immediate vicinity but in the entire county and even much farther beyond.

This then was the post which fell vacant in 1878 and to which William Michael Harty was appointed at the age of twenty-six. Exasperatingly little can now be discovered about William Harty's antecedents beyond the fact that his family had moved from their native Limerick to Dublin when he was still a child. He was a choirboy in Christ Church Cathedral and had organ lessons from Robert Prescott

2

Hillsborough Years

Stewart who was Professor of Music in Dublin University. He held for a time a post as church organist in Dundalk and married Annie Elizabeth Richards, daughter of a soldier named Joseph Hamilton Richards, whom he had met when he had gone to give an 'opening' organ recital in Greystones church where she sang in the choir.[2] The fact that Harty had been invited to Greystones on what was presumably an important occasion suggests that he must have already established himself with some degree of reputation. But nonetheless the sparsity of background information leaves one with the impression that the Hillsborough appointment may have been something in the nature of a 'discovery', a taking a chance on a young man's promise, rather than a recognition of already proven merit.

Admittedly this is a guess, but there is support for it in the fact that this was a time when the affairs of the Downshire family, including the appointment of an organist, were in the hands of Lord Arthur Hill. He was a competent and astute man who took over on the death of his brother the fifth Marquis in 1874 until the coming-of-age of his nephew in 1892, and won for himself a special place in local history through the benevolence and far-sightedness of his régime. Here was exactly the kind of person who would make far-reaching and painstaking enquiries when the need arose to find a new organist, and in this he would certainly have been encouraged and helped by his wife who under her maiden name, Annie Harrison, was having a modest success as a composer of songs. These included the plaintive 'In the gloaming' which became part of Hillsborough's folklore, and the Castle chamber organ on which she played is now a treasured possession of the parish church.[3] In a word the situation was one with obvious potential for benevolent patronage and adventurous assistance to someone young and comparatively unknown. If this is the way it was, it is nice to think that Lady Hill certainly got the most appropriate reward in the later discovery that better songs than she had ever dreamed of were being

---

2. Information from the late Miss Alice Harty.
3. Built by George Pike England, 1795. For a description of the two organs in the church see R. I. Stoupe, *Hillsborough Parish Church: the Organs* (Belfast, 1972).

3

William Harty

Annie Harty née *Richards*

written by a child of her protégé.

When Mr and Mrs Harty arrived in Hillsborough they already had three small children — William, John and Edith. Within a year (on 4 December 1879) a third son, Herbert Hamilton, was born — not in the now familiar Organist's House but in a house near the bottom of the hill in Main Street which they had occupied on their first coming and presently vacated for what was to be their permanent home in Ballynahinch Street. Within the next nine years three more sons (Harold, Fred and Archie) and three more daughters (Alice, Irene and Annie May, who died young) had been added, and the family was complete.

In view of this evident domesticity it is surprising to find that the picture of Mrs Harty given (deftly and beyond doubt) by the village memory is nothing like that of busy maternalism which one would expect. On the contrary she seems to have solidified, in local recollection, to be left to us somewhat like Whistler's mother, sitting for ever and ever in her drawing room on a perpetual summer's afternoon, shades pulled against the bright sunlight, erect in a high-backed chair, up to the chin in silk and lace, occupied endlessly in needlework, and with a curled-up cat at her feet. This is what the old people tell us and it cannot be ignored. But there certainly was another side to the lady, for there is evidence from scraps of letters and recalled conversations that the children were in no doubt about their mother's affection and practical concern. She could always be depended upon to show the needed sympathy when someone had a 'sick cold'. Indeed so great was her fearfulness in the face of anything which could bring danger of any sort to her sons and daughters that one of the things which they remembered in adult life was that they often imposed on her goodness by getting her to write letters of excuse to cover up mitching from school.[4] Perhaps inevitably, as she (and they) grew older she fussed over them somewhat extravagantly, and one discovers signs that a grown man could find it 'a bit much' to be addressed by his old mother as 'my dearest darling' and be warned to watch out for broken glass when he went walking on a beach.[5] But have things ever been different between mothers and

4. Harty mentions 'mitching' (staying away from school) in his Memoir, 5.
5. e.g. letter to H. H. Harty *c*1932.

6

William Harty outside the Organist's House

sons?

Yet the mutual affection was there and it was deep, certainly in her son Herbert who assiduously made material provision for her in her old age and truly mourned her death. One thing her children never forgot was that she was responsible for organizing the annual seaside holiday, which was usually spent in Donaghadee. Apparently this was always very much mother's prerogative and there was great coming-and-going in the Organist's House as Mrs Harty packed the large wicker-work hampers and announced who would travel with her in the train and who would go on bicycles with father. They learnt to walk like troopers — 'Six miles from Bangor to Donaghadee' — and the same distance all the way back. And they learnt to swim — from the Warren to the Pier in long slow strokes. So Mrs Harty was not entirely as aloof from the hurly-burly of family affairs as the recollections of ancient neighbours might make her appear. Maybe it was just a highly-developed sense of propriety that misled them. Or perhaps it was a mixture of things — a feeling that she was 'a southerner' and therefore never entirely at home in the North — and a slightly self-conscious awareness that she was, after all, the organist's wife. Things like these may have given an impression of formality which remained uppermost in the minds of the Hillsborough people, who invariably referred to her as 'Mrs Harty' (as indeed her family usually did!) and would never have dared to call her by her Christian name.

Father was a very different kettle of fish, although indeed in him too there was a certain 'air' which arose in part (it is said) from a deeply cherished conviction that he was the rightful but dispossessed heir to a baronetcy.[6] As far as can be discovered no effort was ever made to substantiate this rumour, but it went well with William Harty's genial benevolence to all and sundry and his acknowledged superiority in the Hillsborough community. As organist he held a very special place in the village hierarchy under the rule of the Castle and the Marquis. In fact, once one counted out the Downshire Agent who lived nearby in a suitably secluded large house (and possibly the Rector?), there just was not anyone in the entire *ménage* who came higher: and this in itself was enough to encompass the holder of the

6. Continuing enquiry into the family background suggests that there may have been some basis for this.

office with a peculiar *je-ne-sais-quoi*. One can only speculate that on occasion when the eating habits of his large brood put a strain on his purse — not to mention his total inability to 'get organized' and Mrs Harty's splendid indifference to the price of anything of which she happened to think the children were in need — William may well have given in to the wish that the rate for the job (£50 *per annum*) could have been a bit more commensurate with the exaltation of his station. And certainly the children must sometimes have had the same wish when they had to take it in turns to feed and bed their father's pony because he could not afford to pay a man to do it.[7]

In fact William had a succession of ponies. He could never resist a change of beast if one took his fancy on a fair day. All that was required in the way of basics was that it should be big enough to pull the trap (shiny black with red-lined wheels) and small enough to fit into the somewhat under-sized stable which had been made out of part of an old cottage which had been incorporated at a right angle into the rear of the Organist's House. But the pony and trap were not everything that William possessed in the line of transport. Indeed it is hard to resist the notion that he may have kept the equipage more or less only for the sake of appearances — and Mrs Harty. He for his part relied heavily on a tricycle that took him high up to near the level of the hedgerows on wheels two feet six inches in radius. He loved his tricycle and cut a dash on a fine day with his dinged black hat, red beard draping his speckled silk waistcoat, tweed trousers and jacket, and black boots. He sat stiffly upright and straight-armed, which threw out the lines of his frontal proportions and left his feet slightly in advance of his body as he thrust on the pedals. And he really could cover the ground: on at least two occasions he went as far as Dublin to attend a *Feis*.

On short journeys within village limits he walked, and every small boy in Hillsborough knew that 'The Fiddler' (as the children called him) was worth watching as he passed down the street. He would stride along with his broad hands clasped behind his back and the shaggy head set at an upward angle as though he were listening for inspiration to come floating down from the house-tops. Then abruptly he would stop, stand stock still with eyes shut, and softly

7. Memoir, 6.

9

whistle eight or nine notes before moving on another ten paces, where the same impromptu recital would be performed again. It was inevitable that the lads of the village should poke fun. But at a discreet distance withal, for this was the age when good manners in the younger generation still could be promoted by the weight of a man's hand, and there are still a few of the old choirboys around who will vouch for it that William Harty's hands could wield a hefty clout.

While on the subject of misdemeanour we may perhaps meet the claims of honest reporting by admitting that there were times in the forty years of William Harty's tenure when the choristers were less than responsive to his leadership. On at least one occasion the Select Vestry had a long discussion on problems of discipline and attendance and at Mr Harty's instigation they introduced a system of fines. At sixpence a time on a salary of £3 or £4 *per annum* it must have constituted a major threat, but nowadays the whole record in all sorts of ways makes very strange reading.

Fortunately such things were but momentary tribulations, mere ripples on the pond of William's tranquillity. Here he was with a devoted wife and happy family, and a job which was as near to being a sinecure as anything could be and yet involve enjoyable work — and with a garden bounded by old stone walls which gave enough shelter for pears and plums, and right in the centre a splendidly exuberant apple tree. Here in the shade he would stretch himself out in the relaxed moments of a summer's day and read a book (think of a tune?) or watch the children play. Indeed, these children seemed to be constantly at play even when they showed an ingrained suspicion of strangers by shouting 'Visitors!' at the top of their lungs at the first ring of the doorbell. They would scuttle into favourite hiding-places in the surrounding shrubbery for all the world like a flock of startled birds, and there they would stay until the 'All Clear'. Then they would re-emerge and the games would begin again: a whole variety of games.[8]

Alice has recalled, for example, the day her father came into the garden unexpectedly and found John and Harold and Edith and the others 'having a funeral'. In fact there was some substance to it (as

8. Memoir, 4.

you might say) for they were burying a cat. It was Mrs Harty's ginger cat that had come to an untimely end through ill-chosen combat with a roving fox terrier. They had the body in a cardboard box 'borne of four'. Harold was in charge of the obsequies, draped in a table cloth and intoning ponderously from what appeared to be a half page from *The Boy's Own Paper*. The rest were mourners, each clad in items borrowed from mother's rag cupboard: all except Bertie, who was three paces in front (what price the Hallé?) playing *Lento* on a tin whistle. The father stopped dumbfounded. Then overcome by laughter he turned quickly away, stuffing a handkerchief into his mouth so that his amusement would not cause offence to the innocence of little children. Bertie saw the shaking shoulders. The music died, and a child's voice came clearly across the width of the garden: 'Poor father! He's crying! And I never knew he even *liked* the cat!'

Down beyond the lower garden gate there was a little plantation known as The Pleasure Ground, and in it a winding pathway bordered by rhododendrons led through a curious little ornamental stone-arched door to the grounds of the church. So house and church — and organ — were linked in such a way that the whole establishment was sitting on virtually the same ground. William Harty could move from his piano in the music room (on the upper floor beside the nursery) to the Snetzler in the west gallery with no more effort than might have been required to put on his overcoat and move a couple of hundred yards along the path under the shadow of splendid forest trees.

It would be an over-simplification to say that he had a fixed daily routine, for there were the interruptions caused by the arrival of pupils at Ballynahinch Street and by excursions into the country to give lessons to the more well-to-do, who would pay a little extra to have tuition for their children in their own homes. For these jaunts the pony-trap seemed more appropriate than the tricycle and one of the boys would be press-ganged to come along and keep an eye on the pony until the job was done. It was in this way that young Bertie made the acquaintance of the son of Dr Thomson of the Dispensary at neighbouring Annahilt. Two little daughters of the house were the pupils who had to be taught and meanwhile outside in the sunshine

Bertie Harty and Willie Thomson would talk away the hour and feed grass to the horse. The friendship thus begun was to last until death.

Choir practices were invariable, of course, and so were morning and evening services on Sundays — *and* Harty's highly individualistic method of conducting a Sunday School class. It consisted of taking the children (his own plus a few of their friends) up to the organ loft on Sunday afternoon and telling them the story of Jesus — with organ accompaniment. Alice Harty has recalled how they all perched precariously on the old oak benches and felt them tremble when William filled the arches of the church with great blasts of sound. He played Handel's 'Messiah' with his own commentary. 'The prophet Isaiah knew of His coming and this is what he said — ''He shall feed His flock...'' ': the section would come to its gentle end and William would glance round his audience catching the eye of each one in turn, as though intent on driving the message for ever into childhood memory. The narrative would be taken up again. 'He was despised and rejected...': the music became plaintive and then gathered strength in a cloud of menace and fear. 'They made Him carry the Cross', William would cry out above the catastrophe of sound. Suddenly, abruptly, without the least warning, the music would stop. And then came a gripping stillness which seemed to contribute an even greater dimension to the tragedy which an instant before had thundered out in the music of the organ. 'This, children,' William would say, his voice low and his head bowed over the keyboard as though it were a grief too ghastly to be borne, 'this is the place where He fell down.'

Moments like these, with his father and the music of Handel, must have made a deep impression on the young Bertie. Surely there was an echo of it all long afterwards when, as Sir Hamilton Harty, he stopped a Hallé rehearsal of 'Messiah' in full flight, handed a book to the soloist and said: 'Go away. Read the words. Read them over and over until you mean every syllable of them. Then you will be able to sing.'[9] Somewhere in behind what a critic was later to describe as 'that extraordinarily Irish cast of countenance'[10] and the dreamy certainties of Hamilton Harty's eyes there was a man of

9. As recounted by the soloist, Isobel Baillie.
10. 'Rathcol' in *The Belfast Telegraph*, 19 February 1943.

another generation seated at an organ and teaching unforgettable things to a small boy.

By and by in the village school (after a brief spell in a kindergarten run in Main Street by a Miss McGifford) it became apparent that young Harty was 'odd'. Not *very* 'odd' for the rough-and-tumble of life with his brothers and sisters, and the need for every one of them to lend a hand with the household chores, was enough to prevent the artistic bent becoming too exuberant. But nonetheless, in the eyes of the other pupils in an average class the lad was far from being ordinary, if only because for as long as any of them could remember he could play the organ in the parish church. You could even hear him occasionally at a Sunday morning service when the Fiddler would move over and let him share the bench. It never sounded as good as when the Fiddler was doing it because his legs were still too short for him to use the pedals. But certainly he could manage a hymn or two, and there was quite a flurry in the school one day when Harty mitched: and this time it was not for bird-nesting! They found him eventually up in the church playing 'There's a friend for little children' — over and over again — during the funeral of a baby who had died of croup. It was remembered that his father brought him home hand in hand.

Then there was the business of 'my mighty orchestra'. He talked of this (unbelievably) from time to time. Once, for example, when a bunch of the village lads met him on the lake walk in the Large Park he was holding a broken-off branch of rhododendron in his hand and flailing it around in the air. 'What are you doing, Bertie?' they asked. The reply was almost predictable but nonetheless highly offensive to the young: 'I'm conducting my mighty orchestra.' The circle was made and closed in. Luckily, the screams and shouts brought rescue for Harty in the shape of a raw-boned youth (of the same age as the rest but impressively bigger) who had appointed himself guardian to Harty at moments when he was being 'picked on' in school. His name, by the way, was Crane — Walter Crane — and he subsequently carved out a distinguished career as a doctor specializing in tuberculosis. When the battle was over and the brigands put to flight the victim picked himself up from the ground where he had been at the bottom of the pile. 'D'ye know, Walter, if

you hadn't come along I do believe I would have been deaded.'
Crane was unimpressed: 'The next time I catch you talking such daft
nonsense there'll be no need for others to thump you,' he said, 'I'll
do it myself.' And he added as he walked away, 'Sometimes I think
you are an ass.'[11] It was early days for the youngster to be learning
some of the hard things that are part of the cost that must be borne
if a man happens to have within him the spark of genius which will
often leave him lonely and misunderstood.

Early days indeed! When Bertie was ten years old he was well
enough on his way to be much in demand (with father *and* mother
who played the violin) for a place in the bill of apparently endless
'Soirées' and 'Grand Concerts' which were held throughout the
countryside. They seem to have been rollicking occasions with an
aftermath of tea and cream buns. His sister Edith was his special
partner, she as violinist and Bertie at the piano. 'I can see her now,'
he wrote long afterwards, 'a little fair girl in a "pinny" and myself,
plump and important, in a "sailor suit" '[12] He also admitted long
afterwards that after one such public appearance a local paper
reported: 'Bertie Harty and his sister Edie played "Gages d'amitie"
and you could have heard them a mile off.'

About this time he undertook his first commission as a teacher, to
the wife of a local tailor. He gave an account of it in a talk to an
Association of Music Teachers in Australia in May 1934.

> She was very shy and evidently thought that a young teacher would be less embarras-
> sing for her. The tailor was not wealthy, and the arrangement made was that for every
> term I taught his wife, the tailor would make me a suit. If my teaching was anything
> like the suit the tailor made for one term's teaching it must have been frightful.

Even if this is not self-deprecatory it is certain that the whole Harty
family and Bertie in particular were involved from earliest childhood
in a continuous round of musical activity. In fact there was virtually
no relaxation from it, apart from what they called 'stable duty' and
times for play, which at the age of nine or ten began to include fierce
bouts of handball against the gable of the Organist's House and ela-
borately-staged bicycle races round the garden. On one significant

11. As told to the author by the late Dr H. A. Maginess and the late Dr Walter
    Crane.
12. Memoir, 8.

occasion it was a race between schoolboys on bicycles and William on his tricycle. But Bertie took the precaution of calling the opposition aside before the start and giving them a strict injunction: 'Go now,' he said, 'ride as fast as you like, but just you remember that no one ever beats my father.'[13]

Father taught everyone and everything — organ, piano, violin, cello and singing.[14] After a hard day spent with his roll of pupils, which by and by spread over a wide area of the countryside, he still found the energy — and the patience — to bring the family together for practice at home. There was the family string quartet consisting of mother and Edith with violins, father with the cello and Bertie with the viola. And everyone in some sort of fashion seems to have been playing the piano all the time. Harty wrote in the Memoir written some forty years later:

[My father] had an unerringly good taste in music and had managed to acquire a large and very complete library, not only of church music and organ music but of oratorios, symphonies, operas, chamber music and of music for piano. His habit was to say — 'There is most of the greatest music that has been written. Play through it, all of it — everything — and at the end you will have gained a good musical education.' For my part I took him at his word and consider the experience thus gained as the basis of any musical powers I may possess.

And in *The Musical Times* (1920) he is quoted as follows:

Music in my early impressions did not mean fiddlers at fairs or immemorial drinking-songs in taverns, or indeed anything more Bohemian or picturesque than my father's organ-playing ... and chamber music at home, where my mother led the family string quartet. I can recall hearing as a small child the sonatas of Mozart and Beethoven being played downstairs as I lay falling asleep.[15]

As though all this were not enough, William Harty ran a Saint Cecilia Choir which successfully blended not only voices but also social strata in the Hillsborough community. A photograph of the choir survives, showing heavily moustached men in high collars and ladies in long draperies and flower-garden hats. He also found time to vent his curiosity in spiritualism, and reports of séances in the Organist's

13. As remembered by the late Dr. H. A. Maginess.
14. He also composed a bit: a Magnificat and Nunc Dimittis by him were published by Novello in 1885, with a dedication to the Marchioness of Downshire.
15. *The Musical Times*, lxi (1920), 227.

I wonder if everyone who after many years looks back
on a distant childhood feels the same half-sad half-
happy emotions that touch me now that I am about
to write of my early days in a ~~village~~
northern Irish village and of the beginnings of a
musical career which began there? I expect that
we do all of us feel the same about our childhood
days, for those were the days of freedom and
lack of care, of hope and confident trust in the
future, of freshness and keen enjoyment of all
the new adventures and experiences which seemed to happen
so frequently in our carefree lives. No doubt ~~our~~
childish ~~days~~ days were tempered with occasional sorrows and
annoyances which we have since forgotten, so that
we now remember only the sunshine and quite
forget the clouds. At least that is my experience
when I recall those early happy days.

There is a small village – a beautiful village in
the County Down, about 12 miles from the city
of Belfast. It was here I was born and
lived until I was 13 or 14: Built, for the most part, on the side

The first page of Harty's unpublished Memoir

16

House brought a pleasant shudder to the susceptible neighbours. And he accumulated a considerable collection of books of Irish poetry and folklore. He loved 'the Gaelic' and passed on to his son both his enthusiasm and his sensitivity for its haunting beauty. This was a family circle in which the 'feeling' of music and literature was in the very air the children breathed. It was less a case of a youngster with the gifts of Hamilton Harty being educated than of his essential core being formed within the structure of the joy of discovery; of having a sort of sublimity stirred in the mind and heart through a dawning awareness of the true significance of reality. Years later when Harty said he had never received any formal musical education, or any real education at all apart from that given to him by his father, he was stating the literal truth. When in the years of public acclaim he talked with deep feeling of his village home and attributed all he had achieved to his father's influence it was in no sense an act of contrived modesty. There was no question of the 'successful' man admitting coyly to 'humble' beginnings. On the contrary, when Harty referred to his father — and to Hillsborough — he was simply sharing his enthusiasm for the richness he had enjoyed and the wonderful things he had known.

Hillsborough, as a place, must get a special mention here for in a remarkable way it provided exactly the sort of background needed for the nurturing of this particular kind of gift in this particular child. The interaction between environment and personality was deep and vital and became as discernible in later life as the stamp of the potter on the clay.

First and obviously, there was the inescapable sense of the presence and the wonder of the world of nature. Here were winding lanes and great trees; lake water in which to fish and swim; boyhood haunts in little islands of solitariness; the call of the thrush in evening and the tumultuous flight of geese in the early morning light.

Harty loved all these things with a love that he never lost. When he was stretched to the limit in his professional career and living in suburban England he would take days off for walking, walking anywhere in all weather and preferably in a place with trees. 'No trees' was the disgruntled comment he scribbled into a guide book which he used to help him to explore an area on the borders of Manchester.

17

It was for him the worst he could have said. When he bought a house at Eccles in Lancashire he called it 'Ballinderry' ('the town of the oakwood') and even took over an adjoining building site so that he could plant it with oaks and limes.

Again, there was humanity in his village, the kindliness of neighbours, the familiarity of small shops, the easy friendships of a tightly-knit community in which there were no strangers.

In this environment Harty unconsciously found his social idiom, his gift of total ease in the company of apparently ill-assorted acquaintances, his genuine and spontaneous care for anyone in need, his sense of personal involvement with those who worked with him. Throughout a life which was often to make him the focus of obsequious adulation and provide him with the place of honour on glittering occasions, he retained a curiously unaffected simplicity. He remained unalterably and totally unashamedly the child of the village, his father's dutiful son.

And there was a striking dimension of 'Irishness' in Hillsborough. At first glance it might seem incongruous to speak thus of 'the borough of the Hills', which was in a sense the very epitome of the process of plantation in which the natives were ejected and the 'strangers' took their place. But despite this and the evidence of English influence on every side there was still a strikingly vivid sense of Irish 'presence'. Basically this was due to the fact that the original planter, Moyses Hill, unlike the general pattern of invasion, had not set out to obliterate the native identity. On the contrary he took a symbolic step in defying the anti-fraternization laws of the time by marrying an Irishwoman, Alice MacDonnell of Dunluce, and being openly boastful of it. From then on this became a consciously-held precedent in the family history and consistently influenced the attitudes and behaviour of the succeeding generations. In another direction we see the deliberate fostering of a sense of heritage in the maintaining of Magennes' fort as a going concern long after it had ceased to have any military importance. Indeed in the late 18th century the old fort was an integral item in Wills Hill's master plan for the new Georgian village and he preserved and adorned it as an historic relic with characteristic disregard of the cost. The same explicit respect for history comes out also in the way in which the Hill

family put what we might call a 'conservation order' on the ruins of
the 7th-century chapel, bringing together the scattered stones in a
manner which can be seen by the visitor to this day. And they carried
over the 12th-century dedication to Saint Malachi for their plantation
church, indicating that they thought of themselves as restorers of the
old rather than builders of the new. Perhaps most indicative of their
independent attitude in an age when contempt for all things Irish
was characteristic of many of their class, is the fact that the Hills took
a pride in recalling that one of Wills' maternal ancestors had raised
the money to finance the first publication of the Old Testament
translated into the Irish language. An inscribed presentation copy of
the first edition was preserved by them as a treasured possession and
is now in the custody of the parish church where it is on permanent
display.

Thus, contrary to what might be the expectation, it is clear that a
child who grew up in Hillsborough in Harty's time was as familiar
with the old native fort, and its story of Irish chieftains and the
echoes of their war cries, as he was with the planter's castle across the
way and the sound of the horses' hooves when the Marquis of Downshire clattered through the entrance gates in his four-in-hand. He
would even have at least a snatch of the Gaelic, for every Hillsborough schoolboy knew that the village's old name was 'Cromlyn',
and that it meant 'the crooked glen'. Certainly there would not be
the smallest possibility of his thinking of himself as anything other
than Irish, specially if he were reared (as Harty was) in a house on the
edge of a street which gave him a ring-side seat at the twice-monthly
fair days. All this is now a thing of the past, but the old people of
the village still recall the colourful and boisterous scene in considerable detail. The cattle and sheep were brought from the surrounding
countryside. By lunch time it would be almost impossible for Mr and
Mrs Harty or any of their brood to go through their front door on
to Ballynahinch Street for the mass of mooing and money-making
invaders. The coffee shop down at the corner would be doing a
roaring trade. And by evening so also would the public houses of
which there was never a short supply in old Hillsborough. It could all
end with a band parade and a clouting of drums and maybe a lone
straggler staggering down the steep pavement of Main Street in their

wake, giving his own variations on what would be to Ulster ears one of the old familiar tunes. Bertie Harty must have watched it all — and heard it all — scores of times. Who knows but maybe even then as he peered out from behind the curtain while the last survivors of the raucous day melted away in the shadows of the dark — maybe even then the seeds were being sown for an Irish Symphony. And if it should seem to the reader to be a distortion of time to ascribe such a mature response to one who was still no more than a child, it shows how possible the improbable can become in such circumstances to discover that he took up his first appointment as a church organist at the age of fourteen.

The parish of Magheragall, about three miles from Hillsborough as the crow flies, gave itself a touch of immortality when the Select Vestry took a chance on the youngster early in 1894. We do not know much about his time there but he himself recorded that if he moved fast enough immediately after the beginning of the sermon he could be up the ladder to the top of the church tower for bird's eggs and down again before the clergyman announced the next hymn. We know also that his father was still keeping an eye on things and now and then he would trot the pony over to Magheragall on a week night and demonstrate for Bertie's benefit how to teach a choir.[16]

In November 1895 he moved to Saint Barnabas' Church in Belfast. Here the pace quickened. An 'excellent local violinist' named T. J. Lindsay befriended him and together they formed a chamber music group. He also got a place in the viola section of an orchestral society and although this in itself was not entirely successful ('I lacked both tone and technique') it enabled him to learn a great deal about orchestral work and gave him confidence to make excursions into composition. He wrote pieces for various instruments, three string quartets and several songs, including 'Sea-Wrack' which he later

16. Magheragall, Select Vestry minutes, 12 February 1894: 'Master Bertie Harty appointed organist at £12 per annum, Mr [William] Harty undertaking to train the choir once a week for £4 in addition'. Mr Harty's commitment was soon reduced to the first six months. The date in the minutes conflicts with Harty's statement (Memoir, 9-10) that he was 'barely 12'. It is possible that he was doing the job unofficially before 1894 since the post was vacant for a long time.

described as having 'achieved a considerable success' [17]

But the first enthusiasm of being in Belfast soon flagged. In the 1890s it was a city preoccupied with industrial expansion and for the most part it had little to offer. Harty decided to move. He was still little more than a child (sixteen years old) but an early tendency to tubbiness had gone and friends recalled him as a presentable young man, five feet nine inches in height, with grey eyes, fair complexion, and an unruly lock of dark brown hair. He happened to see an advertisement for an organist and choirmaster in Christ Church, Bray. He applied and he was appointed. God knows what they would say when they found out the statistical truth about what people call 'experience'! But anyway it would be new ground and a real beginning, and however it turned out it could at least be said for the place that it was near the mountains and the sea. It cannot have been hard to pack the bag for there was very little to put into it except essential clothes, maybe a bundle of manuscripts with scribbled notes for a song. And there were two photographs: one was of the Organist's House in Hillsborough and the other of his mother, showing her seated in the garden with a huge Persian cat on her lap. He kept them always ever after. There is no record of William having made any contribution: maybe he paid the fare. Anyway it is likely that Bertie was even then aware of the truth which by and by he would tell the world — that his father had given him already all that he had, and all that he ever would become.

17. Memoir, 10-11.

Drawing by Harold Speed, 1905
(Courtesy of the National Gallery of Ireland)

II DUBLIN AND LONDON

Philip Hammond

At Christ Church, Bray, Harty had the advantage of working with a senior curate, the Reverend Digby Scott, who had a considerable knowledge of music, both sacred and secular, and an instinctive sympathy with a young man still uncertain of his path. More importantly however he came into contact with a much wider field of musical experience, which had previously been restricted by the narrow outlets provided in the North of Ireland at that time. As Bray is situated just south of Dublin, Harty was able to take full advantage of the musical circles which had begun to flourish in the capital under the leadership of Commendatore Michele Esposito (1855-1929), a Neapolitan who had been appointed professor of piano at the Royal Irish Academy of Music in 1882. A man of great personality and broad musical interests, being himself conductor, pianist, violinist, composer and publisher, Esposito was then the leading light in Dublin musical life. He founded a small symphony orchestra — the Dublin Orchestral Society — organized frequent chamber music recitals for the Royal Dublin Society, and in order that the Academy would influence the standard of teaching throughout the country, he established a plan of local centre examinations in 1894. Perhaps his most enduring achievement was the foundation of a school of piano playing at the Academy, a tradition which is still carried on there by his pupils. For his services to music in Ireland he was awarded an Honorary Doctorate by Trinity College in 1905.

Harty soon managed to make the acquaintance of Esposito, who thereafter seemed to take the place of his father with respect to musical guidance and assistance. This association grew into a lifelong and close friendship, and Harty came to regard him with the greatest respect and even reverence.

...at Dublin I fell willingly captive to Dr Michel[e] Esposito. This Italian musician is the presiding genius of all that there is of music in Ireland. As an all-round musician

Michele Esposito (oil portrait)

Dublin and London

he is, I should say, unsurpassed in Europe. I send him for criticism everything I write, and put as implicit faith in him now as when a boy — he has always been right.[1]

Contrary to what is often thought, Harty was never a pupil of Esposito in the formal sense of the word, but as he said when unveiling a portrait of him in Dublin in 1926, he 'never ceased to learn from him and to regard him as his revered master'[2] One of the standing jokes between the two men was Esposito's refusal to give Harty piano lessons. Harty recounts that he first met Esposito entering a train at Bray station; on asking to be taken on as a piano pupil, Esposito replied 'Show me your hands — no they are not good for piano — the thumbs are too short!'[3] In spite of this seemingly insurmountable impediment, Harty concentrated very much on studying the piano and began to acquire an enviable reputation in that particular field. As he explained at a later date in a talk entitled *The Art of Pianoforte Accompaniment*, the circumstances of his early life led him to gravitate more towards accompaniment than to a career as a solo performer:

As a boy in a little village in Ireland I was lucky in having certain musical advantages, but not that of highly specialised piano teaching. On the other hand there was in my home a comprehensive library of music of all kinds, and in learning what could be taught locally as regards piano playing (and I may add Organ playing) I found great interest in playing through this great mass of varied music. But of the higher branches of pianoforte technique I knew little. In the end I was thrown on my own resources to acquire the necessary technique of a solo pianist. I know now that the highest skill is not to be acquired in this way, but I did not know it then, and though my efforts were immense, the end of it all was disappointment as far as being a solo pianist was concerned. But in missing the goal in one direction certain qualities had been acquired which served me well later on as a player of piano accompaniments... They were — an all round kind of technique, not brilliant in any one way but fairly sound — a capacity of reading at sight which was unusual — and a very wide and comprehensive acquaintance with music of all kinds and conditions — not piano music particularly, but music for the Church, music for the Stage, Chamber music, Vocal music, Orchestral music, everything of which there was a copy in the library... Then at different times I learnt to play, if only a little, upon the Viola, the 'Cello, the Horn and the Cornet — not with the idea of becoming in any way expert upon these instruments, but simply that I

1. *The Musical Times*, lxi (1920), 227-28. Esposito's gravestone at Trespiano has inscribed on it three bars of music by 'H.H.'
2. Newspaper report, Scrapbook A, 4.
3. Memoir, 14; also mentioned in *The Musical Times, loc cit.*

might get a good knowledge of the different clefs and of the transposing instruments. This brought a certain ease and facility in transferring orchestral score to the Piano...

When I discovered that to be a first class solo pianist required special gifts, and special training, I conceived the idea of trying to be a specialist in pianoforte accompaniment. Wide though badly organised study had at least developed many aptitudes which were of the greatest help and importance in the branch to which I devoted myself for a number of years. [4]

Harty's increasing reputation as an accompanist led to his being invited to undertake many engagements in this field, and it was through his great skill in this art that he first came prominently before public attention in Dublin. He was 'very much in demand at all the important concerts and consequently he won the good graces of all the foremost singers and performers'. [5] On one occasion he was asked to accompany Madame Ella Russell, one of the outstanding singers of the day. This event took place at Vice-Regal Lodge, Dublin, during Queen Victoria's last official visit to Ireland. She was so impressed by Harty's playing that she subsequently presented him with a jewelled scarf-pin.

At this time also, he became associated with the *Feis Ceoil* in Dublin, which had been inaugurated in May 1897 on the basis of a festival competition. He later became official accompanist for the *Feis* and in this capacity made the acquaintance of John McCormack, when the latter made his first appearance there. This festival also provided an outlet for another facet of Harty's talents — that of composition. His String Quartet in F (op.1) received one of the highest awards in the 1900 *Feis* and was warmly praised in the *Weekly Irish Times*.[6] The following year he won another prize with his Fantasiestücke for violin, cello and piano (op.3), and this run of successes continued for the next few years.[7]

However, in spite of the many opportunities afforded to him in Dublin, the young musician began to feel that his future career lay elsewhere. As his reputation as an accompanist grew he was engaged for tours of the principal cities of Great Britain; and artists whom he

4. Typescript, 3. In all quotations the original spelling, punctuation and capitals have been retained.
5. *Weekly Irish Times*, 7 July 1900.
6. *Weekly Irish Times*, 7 July 1900.
7. See p. 28.

met — notably the cellist W. H. Squire, with whom he maintained a lifelong friendship — encouraged him to think seriously of making his career in London.[8] He was wary of falling into the same trap that ensnared many fellow Irish musicians, as he later remarked:

> ...The Irish musical student is greatly facile, and still more greatly indolent. He reaches a certain point and then drifts. Ireland offers him no scope; yet, as a rule, he is reluctant to leave home. [9]

This did not hold good with Harty. In January 1901 he tendered his resignation as organist at Bray, having been offered a similar post at All Saints Church, Norfolk Square, London. This appointment would, he hoped, provide him with a base in one of the main musical centres of the world, and offer him the wider scope for his activities, which both his talents and ambition demanded.

* * *

Harty's early days in London were marked by a rapid rise to public recognition through his great gifts as an accompanist. Unfortunately the church position lasted only a week: apparently there was some disagreement between himself and the Vicar, who did not altogether approve of his organ-playing! However, with the help of W. H. Squire, he was able at first to subsist on fees gained by playing at high-society musical soirées. It was not long before he received engagements from more professional bodies, and among the first of these was accompanying at the Boosey 'Ballad Concerts'; these ran from 1867 to 1927 and featured not only the finest singers of the period but instrumentalists of the highest calibre such as Pachmann, Backhaus, Kreisler, Szigeti, Suggia and Solomon. He also appeared regularly at the South Place Sunday Popular Concerts, where many of his smaller compositions received performances. It was here in 1904 that his String Quartet in A was given its first London performance. Through his work as an accompanist he came into contact with

---

8. Memoir, 21-2. Harty's Romance & Scherzo (1903) and Two Pieces (1907) for cello and piano were dedicated to Squire. They made several recordings together between 1926 and 1930 (see Discography).
9. *The Musical Times*, lxi (1920), 228.

many of the leading singers of the day. One of these was the soprano Agnes Nicholls, who had made her operatic début in 1895, at the age of eighteen, as Dido in Purcell's 'Dido and Aeneas'. Her career flourished in the late 1890s and in 1901 she first appeared at Covent Garden as the Dew Fairy in 'Hansel and Gretel'. They met in the autumn of 1902 and were married two years later. As a musical partnership Agnes Nicholls and Hamilton Harty were perfectly matched — but their marriage was not a success. The reasons for the failure are irrelevant: to seek them would be an impertinence; to state them if they could be found would be an offence against the memory of a man who regarded respect for the privacy of others as the very essence of good manners. From a practical point of view, however, the marriage had important consequences for Harty. Although he was making a name for himself as an accompanist his main ambition was to be a conductor, and his wife was of considerable assistance to him in his attempts to gain recognition from important figures in the musical world of London. Agnes Nicholls indeed had very influential friends, one of them being Hans Richter, the most eminent conductor in England of his day. It was through him that Harty later gained his first important engagement as conductor.

These early years in London were his most fruitful period as a composer. As we have seen, before moving to London he had begun entering works for the *Feis Ceoil* in Dublin, and he continued to do so after he had left Ireland: he won prizes with the String Quartet in A (op.5), 1902, the Piano Quintet in F (op.12), 1904, and in the same year with his Irish Symphony. This last work makes use of a number of Irish melodies and he once said of it:

Since I was a boy at Hillsborough ... I always had the idea of writing something in which I would try to get the 'flavour' of village life there, and the legends associated with the district and province. Although I have not explained it in words, the 'Irish Symphony' is really an autobiography, and I have no doubt that others used to the country will recognise many of the allusions. [10]

This work was to feature in concert programmes throughout his life, and he revised it at least twice. The first performance in 1904 was of

10. Quoted in an obituary notice, Scrapbook D, 11.

added significance in that it was also the first occasion on which Harty conducted an orchestra.[11] In 1907 his Comedy Overture was given its first performance at a Queen's Hall Promenade Concert; and in December the same year his setting for soprano and orchestra of Keats's 'Ode to a Nightingale' (op.16) was first performed at the Cardiff Festival, sung by his wife, to whom it was dedicated. Another important work of these years was the Violin Concerto, composed in 1908 and first performed by Joseph Szigeti and the New Symphony Orchestra in 1909 at the Queen's Hall. Szigeti later wrote about this work in his autobiography *With Strings Attached*:

> The earliest of my many associations with composers came before I was twenty, with the concerto which Hamilton Harty dedicated 'To Joska Szigeti, in Friendship', and which I suspect set the pattern for my subsequent approach to other such tasks. For I think more and more that one's whole musical make-up is conditioned by some such early experience from which is evolved the 'working method' that serves one in the most diverse tasks, and at different stages of development... Harty was then — around 1908 — England's premier accompanist; and my working at his manuscript concerto, with him at the piano coaxing out of his instrument all the orchestral colour which he had dreamed into his score, was probably decisive in forming what a long-suffering and excellent pianistic partner of mine later on termed my 'expensive tastes' in accompanying.

Szigeti subsequently performed the concerto a great many times, in Great Britain and abroad.[12] During the first decade of the century Harty also published a considerable number of songs, including some of his best-known ones: 'Sea-Wrack' and 'Three Traditional Ulster Airs' ('The Blue Hills of Antrim', 'My Lagan Love' and 'Black Sheela of the Silver Eye'), 1905; 'Lane o' the Thrushes', 1907; and 'Six Songs of Ireland', 1908. However, it is possible that some of these were composed considerably earlier — like 'Sea-Wrack', which (as we have seen) goes back to his Hillsborough days.

It is worthwhile recording that in composition — as in other aspects of music — Harty was almost entirely self-taught. In matters such as orchestration for example, his method was one of studying the works of the great masters and learning from these. Elgar comes

11. Memoir, 18. See also *The Musical Times*, xlv (1904), 396, and xlvi (1905), 405.
12. Joseph Szigeti, *With Strings Attached: Reminiscences and Reflections* (London, 1949), 107-8.

Dublin and London

to mind as another master of orchestration who was largely self-taught. But being an autodidact can have its drawbacks: academic training may move on well-defined and sometimes restrictive lines, but at the very least it does provide opportunities to encounter the new ideas and new sounds of other young musicians. Harty missed out on this, and by the time he reached London his tastes and predilections were firmly set and did not alter to any great extent in the after-years. He was an intuitive composer, a product of the Romantic tradition: as we shall see later, he abhorred the merely 'logical' in music, and 'the terrible cleverness of the moderns'. As Neville Cardus wrote, '[Harty's] music, always composed with a civilised touch, did not vaunt itself in any "avant garde" directions. He was content to compose for pleasure, out of love of sound considered good to hear in his day.'[13]

Harty's career as a conductor received a great boost in March 1911 when Richter asked him to conduct his latest composition, the tone poem 'With the Wild Geese', at a London Symphony Orchestra concert.[14] As a result of this and other concerts, he was engaged as one of two new conductors — Safonoff being the other — for the 1912-13 season of LSO concerts at the Queen's Hall. Among the works that Harty conducted was his own Variations on a Dublin Air which received its first performance in February 1913. However at the orchestra's Annual General Meeting in July that year the chairman regretfully reported that the concerts conducted by Harty had made a financial loss (so had those conducted by Elgar!); consequently he was not engaged for the next season. Fortunately, through his friendship with Esposito, he was engaged to share the conducting of a series of concerts in Dublin during August of 1913, the orchestra for which strangely enough comprised fifty-two members of the LSO.[15] During this series he conducted his Irish Symphony.

The work, however, which helped more than any other to establish

13. From a sleeve-note for a recording of Harty's Piano Concerto on HSL 106.
14. Composed in 1910 and first performed at the Cardiff Festival that year.
15. This series was promoted by Sir Stanley Cochrane, a leading Irish businessman whom Harty had known since his years in Bray. Cochrane and Esposito founded a music publishing firm, C. E. Music Publishers, which published some of Harty's music.

Dublin and London

Harty among the foremost British composers was 'The Mystic Trumpeter', commissioned by the Leeds Festival and first performed there in October 1913. This was a setting for baritone, chorus and orchestra of a poem by Walt Whitman, a poet whose universal and pantheistic vision appealed to several composers of that time, Delius and Vaughan Williams among them.[16]

In 1913 Harty had his first experience of conducting opera, when he directed 'Tristan and Isolde' and 'Carmen' at Covent Garden. Although new to opera he acquitted himself with credit; but he never had much feeling for this branch of music, as he later made clear in an interview for *The Musical Times*.[17] His preference and ambitions were most definitely for the concert platform, and it was in this sphere that he continued to be more and more in demand. In January 1914 he conducted the Liverpool Philharmonic Orchestra in a programme which included 'With the Wild Geese' and Rakhmaninov's Piano Concerto no.2, with the composer as soloist. In April the Hallé Orchestra engaged him for the first time, for a performance of 'The Mystic Trumpeter' at the Westmoreland Festival. Around this time he was beginning to become more associated with orchestras in the North of England, and with the outbreak of war more work of this kind came his way. This was because Michael Balling, the German conductor of the Hallé, was out of the country when the war started, and was prevented by the state of hostilities from returning. Thus, his numerous concert engagements in the North had to be distributed among others, including Harty. After a Hallé concert in January 1915 *The Musical Times* had this to say:

Probably by now, as a result of the last few years having brought so many new conductors here, the Manchester public is better qualified than usual to pass judgment on the capacities of these visitors, and if asked to draw up a list of the most meritorious names, that of Mr. Hamilton Harty would be found high up on the list. Orchestral players are probably shrewd judges, too, of whether a man 'has it in him', and their playing under some men has a greater warmth and freedom as compared with their performance under others quite as well endowed in a purely musical sense. Mr. Harty undoubtedly is gifted with a magnetic personality and does not harry his players

16. Reviewed in *The Musical Times*, liv (1913), 744.
17. *The Musical Times*, lxi (1920), 229.

Harty in the Royal Naval Volunteer Reserve, c 1917

needlessly; altogether he is uncommonly well-equipped, and nobody endows music with greater rhythmical life.[18]

In June 1916 he joined the Royal Naval Volunteer Reserve and was posted to hydrophone duties in the North Sea.[19] He was given a temporary commission with the rank of Sub-lieutenant in September 1916, and promoted to Lieutenant the following year. However although these naval duties were very much on a part-time basis and his musical career continued, albeit on a reduced level, the strain of combining these several activities did take its toll on his health, and added to this was the death of his father in February 1918, a loss he felt deeply. In June 1918 he left the RNVR: he seems to have enjoyed his two years in the navy and did not regard it as time wasted. According to his Service Record he displayed 'excellent abilities and diligence'.

By the autumn of 1918 he was sufficiently recovered to resume his work as conductor and accompanist. That December Beecham was prevented by illness from conducting the annual Hallé performance of 'Messiah'. Harty took his place and thereby followed in line with Richter, Balling, Beecham (and later Barbirolli), all of whom made their first conducting acquaintance with this work at the Hallé. Harty adhered to Beecham's plan of omissions and re-ordering of movements, which included the placing of the Hallelujah chorus at the end.[20] He also stood in for Beecham in a performance of Bach's B minor Mass given by the Hallé on 27 March 1919, and again a few days later by the Birmingham Festival Choir. *The Musical Times* remarked that although he took over the work at short notice he showed that 'he knew his Bach score at least as well as some of the orchestral scores which he plays so supremely well'.[21] Harty indeed had a great capacity for acquainting himself with a work almost at a glance, and this was to stand him in good stead in the years ahead, when concerts often had to be put on with little or no rehearsal.

18. *The Musical Times*, lvi (1915), 174.
19. His annotated copy of instructions in the use of the hydrophone still survives.
20. *The Musical Times*, lx (1919), 87.
21. *The Musical Times*, lx (1919), 243.

Harty on his appointment to the Hallé Orchestra, 1920

III THE HALLÉ YEARS AND AFTER

Philip Hammond

In December 1919 an important meeting of the Hallé Society took place to discuss the future of the orchestra. Apart from the severe financial difficulties and resultant disputes between the players and the committee, the question of a permanent conductor was debated at length. Both Beecham and Albert Coates strongly urged the appointment of Harty.[1] As it happened there were few other conductors in England at that time who could have taken a permanent post such as that offered by the Hallé, and to have approached foreign conductors was out of the question, due to the general feeling after the war. Harty realized the opportunities being offered to him and accepted the position.[2]

With the announcement of his appointment, in April 1920 Harty gave one of the few extended personal interviews of his career to *The Musical Times*.[3] Although as a rule he shunned publicity of this sort,[4] this interview is a most revealing exposition and provides many insights into his tastes and attitudes.

Berlioz and Mozart are my private deities. I cannot always make people see what ground they have in common, yet it is clear to me that they are the two great intuitive composers as distinguished from the great logical ones. Of course all great composers must have intuition, but most have had to eke theirs out with logic, while intuition hardly ever seems to have failed my two heroes. And it is intuition that I count as the supreme thing in music. Call it heart against head if you will. In Berlioz, as in Mozart, you are always coming upon a beautiful, fresh-sprung melodic line such as no amount of head-work could have suggested. In Wagner, much as I love his music, I feel sometimes a mechanical process at work which makes me rate him below Berlioz.

This logic that can go on for ever, though intuition fail, is the source of all the dull,

1. See John F. Russell, 'Hamilton Harty', *Music & Letters*, xxii (1941), 216.
2. Concerning Harty's association with the Hallé see C. B. Rees, *100 Years of the Hallé* (London, 1957), and Michael Kennedy, *The Hallé Tradition* (Manchester, 1960).
3. *The Musical Times*, lxi (1920), 227-30.
4. Rees, *op cit*, 67, cites one instance of Harty's reluctance to be interviewed.

pretentious music of the ancients and of the terrible cleverness of the moderns. But I think the modern logicians have the better of it, because they are not so praeter-naturally solemn. Logic if tolerable must tend towards comedy, and such composers as Stravinsky and Ravel (whom I admire greatly) are all that is witty. Save us from the composers who argue solemnly!

He then airs some of his musical antipathies. Opera comes in for an extended attack, and then he moves on to individual composers: 'I confess to finding something weak in Franck's mystical style.' He is equivocal about Brahms, preferring 'the Brahms of Resignation'. Of Scriabin (much in vogue at that time due largely to the advocacy of Albert Coates) he says 'Scriabin — dare I say it? — is not a composer I wholly believe in.' He is appropriately complimentary about the Hallé and Manchester audiences:

The Hallé is the alertest of bands. Its wind is the most beautiful in the country, and the leader, Mr. Catterall, I hold to be the best of our native violinists. Inevitably the Orchestra suffered during the war, and as much as anything from being pulled first this way, then that, by incessant changes of conductors. Of course I shall not be going to them as a stranger. I have no apprehensions, for I know that though there is no possible bluffing of such a first-rate orchestra, and no bullying, they can be got to do anything if one will explain himself quietly and rationally.

In my work I shall come in touch too with various choral societies, and here a thorny problem exists which to my mind has hardly been satisfactorily handled in the past. The problem concerns the relations of the choirmaster who trains the singers and the conductor who directs the public performance. If performances of the larger and more modern choral works are to be brought nearer adequacy, the conductor must in future have more say in the preparation of the choir.

One of the pleasures of the musician at Manchester is in the subtlety of the audiences there. Yes, they are not only keen but also subtle. The difference is immense between them and Londoners, who so often seem to be listening with closed minds. A London audience is often simply not to be won, but sits in apathy as much as to say that as a sufficient impression of such and such a composer, or such and such a work had been formed years ago, no fresh one is desirable. I should despair of charming London with Berlioz in the way in which Manchester has lately been charmed...

My ideal at Manchester will be to have no music played simply because it is new — or because old — or because it is familiar or because not, or just because it was composed in England or in Jugo-Slavia, or in the Isle of Man. I hope to arrange programmes based on worth. I do not believe in too great a proportion of a concert being in strange, novel idioms. I hope to have something new at each concert, and also at each a solid proportion of music that can be enjoyed without the learning of a new language every week.

36

The Hallé Years and After

In the late summer of 1920 Harty went to Manchester to make final arrangements for the forthcoming Hallé season: less than six weeks remained before the opening concert but only forty-three of the seventy-two contracts issued to players had been accepted, and not a single programme had been planned. His first priority was naturally the completion of the orchestra and in this process he raised a storm of protest which grew to national proportions, because he preferred an all-male band of players, which was the tradition with most of the leading orchestras of the time. Despite the difficulties, the sixty-third Hallé season opened on 14 October with the orchestra approaching pre-war size — the only female member being the harpist.

Whilst being fully committed to the Hallé, Harty was also to find time to appear as guest conductor in many other musical centres in Britain and Ireland. There was however little opportunity for composition. The 'Fantasy Scenes from an Eastern Romance' was performed at a Hallé concert in December 1920, having first been heard at a Leeds Saturday Orchestral Concert in January of that year. During the summer of 1922, while on holiday with the Espositos at Fiesole in Italy, he wrote his Piano Concerto in B minor which was first performed in November 1922 at Leeds, and again at Manchester in March 1923, with Beecham conducting and Harty at the piano. Apart from revisions of the Violin Concerto and the Irish Symphony, little else dates from the early period with the Hallé except the orchestral transcriptions of Handel's 'Water Music' (first performed by the Hallé in November 1920) and the 'Music for the Royal Fireworks' (1923).

From the beginning Harty took an interest in the business affairs of the Hallé Society. One early instance of this was his advocacy of municipal aid. Due to the ever-present strain on the financial resources of the Society, the question of municipal subsidies had been much in the forefront of public attention since 1920. Harty re-approached the subject at the Hallé AGM of 1922, asking directly for a corporation grant of £1,000 on the grounds that the Hallé Society was a public institution. Although other such schemes were already in existence in Birmingham and Glasgow, the proposal was at first rejected by the City Council. The issue however reached a successful conclusion in 1924, and municipal concerts survived until 1940, when the second World War put an end to them once and for all.[5]

In these first years with the Hallé it seemed to many that Harty had restored a sense of purpose and interest to the Society, with important repercussions in Manchester and indeed throughout the North of England. The expansion of the number of chamber music recitals was one notable feature. In his role as pianist, Harty and the Catterall Quartet inaugurated the 'Manchester Chamber Concerts', the first of which took place in December 1921, and he also frequently appeared with other groups formed from the Hallé Orchestra. The 'Harty Chamber Concerts', for example, which took place during the 1924-5 season were undertaken with the express purpose of helping and encouraging younger Hallé members who had formed their own ensembles.

In October and November 1924 and January 1925, the Hallé gave three concerts at the Queen's Hall in London. These were planned in collaboration with the Columbia Gramophone Company, to whom Harty had been musical adviser for some years. Although Harty was no stranger to London audiences, this was the first time the Hallé had been in the capital since 1913. The critics were lavish in their praise:

A public that cannot recognize the beauty of well-shaped phrasing, of living rhythm, of balance of instrument with instrument, and blend of strings, wood, and brass, as sections and with one another, of continuity ... of precision in attack, and of the other qualities, small and big, which the Hallé players and Hamilton Harty give us, is incapable of realising that in them it possesses exponents of the very highest class.[6]

Many felt that London had nothing to compare with the Hallé — a situation Harty blamed on the lack of permanent conductors and more especially upon the disruptive practice of players sending along deputies when it suited them. The past four years had inevitably produced results which had benefited both the Hallé and Harty. By now the impetuous urge of his temperament was more under

5. It was as a result of one of these municipal concerts (4 March 1929) that Harty made his famous Columbia recording of 'Nymphs and Shepherds', with the Hallé Orchestra and a choir of Manchester schoolchildren. The recording has recently been re-issued (see Discography), and in 1975 there was a reunion of the 'children' who took part in the original recording.

6. *The Musical Times*, lxvi (1925), 62.

control, and the orchestra in turn had attained a discipline to the point where its responsiveness to Harty's wishes and occasional caprices seemed intuitive. Further visits to the capital took place. One of these (in 1928) occurred shortly after a tour by the Berlin Philharmonic Orchestra: Harvey Grace was moved to assert that 'If (as the Jeremiahs affirm) an occasional visit by a crack orchestra is necessary in order that London may not forget what high-grade playing is like, there is no need to send to the Continent. Manchester is good enough.'[7] As a result of this enthusiastic reception Harty decided to run his own series of concerts at the Queen's Hall. The 'Hamilton Harty Symphony Concerts' lasted for two seasons — 1929-30 and 1930-31 — and each series consisted of six concerts, held on Friday nights to avoid conflict with the regular Manchester Hallé concerts, held on Thursdays. But in spite of the acclamation with which the series were received, finances were to prove too much of a liability. The resultant loss amounted to over £3,000, the whole of which was borne by Harty himself — and after each season he treated the entire orchestra to supper at Pagani's.

Throughout the years, by his subtle and frequently unorthodox approach, which included many flashes of quick mordant wit, Harty built up a very personal relationship with the Hallé.

Many of his privileged artists he called by their Christian names. With most conductors such familiarities would be dangerous, but Harty is an exception. His use of Christian names is typical of the intimate way in which he works.[8]

He regarded each member of his orchestra as a separate human entity and at times 'seemed to exercise something like a Svengalian influence over a player, giving him a sense of artistry that he was not able or willing to put forth for any other conductor'[9] This was not done by any exaggeration of movement or gesture, for in his style of conducting Harty was quiet and undemonstrative. The sway he held in performance stemmed more from facial than body movement, and from his eyes in particular. He always relied upon gaining the interest of his players rather than upon strict discipline, although he

7. *The Musical Times*, lxix (1928), 165.
8. Bernard Shore, *The Orchestra Speaks* (London, 1938), 97.
9. Shore, *op cit*, 95.

would not tolerate slackness or inefficiency in any degree: '... woe betide the player who did not give his utmost! A few quiet words from Harty could be a soul-shrivelling experience'.[10]

During the 1920s official recognition of his achievements came in abundance: a Fellowship of the Royal College of Music (1924), Honorary Doctorates in Music from Trinity College, Dublin (1925) and Manchester University (1926), and above all a knighthood (1925). And others were to follow. But despite the successes, the broadening of the Hallé repertoire and the increase of its strength and reputation, criticism in Manchester about the lack of modern works and frequent changes to the advertized programme had steadily been growing since 1926. Harty's views on contemporary music were well-known, and in 1929 he gave a lecture entitled 'Some Problems of Modern Music', some extracts from which should make his position clear.

Most of us were born towards the close of a wonderfully lively time in music — a period which might be expressed by the formula Bach-Mozart-Beethoven-Brahms-Wagner. Strauss and Elgar are still with us and as far as one can see are the end of that particular line. It is natural that our convictions and outlook should be solidly based on that foundation... On the other hand the bright young people of today deride these composers and make no secret of the fact that they consider them thoroughly boring and out-of-date. They profess to find pleasure and satisfaction in certain latter day developments which an older school finds meaningless and ugly... Are we of an older musical conviction old fashioned and so set in our ways that we are incapable of appreciating the genius and orginality which we are told resides in the works of certain notorious modern composers? Or ... is it not possible that music has ... wandered aside into barren and unfruitful wastes?[11]

Although Harty was obviously of the latter opinion, there was a reasonable representation of other living composers in his programmes, including Bliss, Honegger, Medtner, Lambert, Křenek, Stravinsky, Prokofiev, Vaughan Williams, Bartók and Sibelius. There was however still room for criticism, and Neville Cardus wrote in the *Manchester Guardian* in 1928: 'Why do we get, more often than not, the second-rate things in modern music at the Hallé Concerts nowadays? Why is Atterberg played to us and Bryson and Hely-

10. Maurice Ward, 'Sir Hamilton Harty — an Appreciation', *London Philharmonic Post*, March 1941. Both Maurice Ward and Bernard Shore played under Harty.
11. From Harty's handwritten lecture notes.

SIR HAMILTON HARTY
A caricature by the late Oswald Barrett ('Batt'), drawn in 1928

Caricature by Oswald Barrett ('Batt')

Hutchinson and Goldmark, while the really big men are neglected?'[12] Harty was needled by such criticism, and indeed frequently took exception to Cardus's remarks. However, the two eventually became good friends, though always 'ready to join issue in private or public, at the slightest provocation'[13] Although there were many others who supported him in his views on modern music,[14] Harty decided to reply to his critics, and in an interview for the Manchester edition of the *Daily Express* on 25 May 1929 he had this to say:

I know I have been accused in the past of neglecting modern works which Manchester people have a right to hear, and preserving a too conservative outlook... Previously I have been afraid, partly because I did not think the modern works as good as that music which for convenience we call classical, and partly because I did not feel that the Hallé Society could afford to risk experiments. However, we are going to take our chance. (Quoted in *The Musical Times*, July 1929, 639.)

The 1929-30 season accordingly offered a much more balanced mixture of established classics and less familiar works. Among the latter were Walton's 'Façade' suite (conducted by the composer), Sibelius's Fourth and Fifth Symphonies and Violin Concerto, Vaughan Williams's Pastoral Symphony, Mahler's Ninth Symphony (first performance in England) and Křenek's 'Potpourri'. Choral works were Rakhmaninov's 'The Bells', Kodaly's 'Psalmus Hungaricus' and Constant Lambert's 'Rio Grande'. And the three seasons after that (1930-33) also had a more modern look to them, including Sibelius's First, Third and Seventh Symphonies and 'Tapiola', Prokofiev's Third Piano Concerto, Mahler's 'Song of the Earth', Walton's Viola Concerto and 'Belshazzar's Feast', Shostakovich's First Symphony, and Bax's First and Third Symphonies.

Harty's advocacy of Berlioz, it should be said, was constant over the years, and it was in Berlioz's music that he gave some of his most dazzling performances: 'Faust' (1920), the 'Symphonie fantastique', 'Harold in Italy' (1922), 'Symphonie funèbre et triomphale' (1923), 'Grande messe des morts' (1925 and 1926, including a much-publicized performance in one of the BBC's 'National Concerts' in

12. Quoted by Kennedy, *op cit*, 229.
13. Neville Cardus, *Autobiography* (London, 1947), 222.
14. See letter by John F. Russell, *The Musical Times*, lxx (1929), 446.

the Albert Hall), 'Romeo and Juliet' (1927), 'Les Troyens' (1928). One peculiarity of Harty's programme-building during the Hallé years — his penchant for modern Italian composers (Busoni, Pizzetti, Casella, Respighi) — stems from his friendship with Esposito.

In August 1930 he became the centre of yet another controversy following a presidential address entitled 'Music and the Wireless' which he gave to the Incorporated Association of Organists. In this he launched a scathing attack on the BBC — 'the amiable bandits of Savoy Hill' as he called them — who had recently constituted a new orchestra. Whatever its powers or the honesty of its motives, Harty felt that it was morally wrong and indefensible for the BBC to enter into direct competition with private interests, and a misuse of public funds to expend vast sums on the creation of a new orchestra when better results could be obtained from subsidizing those already in existence. He further claimed that the BBC's growing assumption of autocracy and its tendency to centralize music were not in the best interests of the art, its general music policy 'amateurish and arrogant', awakening the dislike and resentment of most musicians. On a more personal level, Harty had been angered by the way in which the Corporation had not advertized positions in its new orchestra but had approached individual players directly, notably several of his own.

In the summer of 1931 he went on his first American tour. He was much impressed by musical life in the United States and felt it was superior in many ways to that in England, especially in the matter of financial support. On his return he entered academic fields for the first time, having been appointed to give the James W. Alsop Lectures at Liverpool University. In these he dealt with the history and growth of the orchestra, its various components, and conductors and conducting. It was clear however that he was becoming dissatisfied with many aspects of his career in Manchester, and began to see that his future could by no means be restricted by the boundaries of his own country. And his mood cannot have been helped by the hostile reception that Neville Cardus gave one of his American imports, Gershwin's 'An American in Paris', which was performed at the opening concert of the 1931-32 season. But as always he never felt the need or desire to explain his motives and perhaps it was due

Farewell Concert with the Hallé Orchestra, 1933

to a lack of communication that many of the misunderstandings and controversies arose. Stephen Williams once wrote:

In some ways Sir Hamilton is an enigma. He lives a lonely life in a house in Eccles. He shuns publicity, he affects the utmost fastidiousness in his way of life. He is an utterly charming man to meet, yet one can never be sure what subtle thoughts are lurking behind that bland expansive smile. A great musician, and a fascinating, bafflingly complex man.[15]

When Harty returned from a second American tour in the late summer of 1932 it was announced that he had been appointed Artistic Adviser and Conductor-in-chief of the London Symphony Orchestra.[16] The Hallé committee, however, was most concerned at this news, and although Harty pointed out that his contract contained no barring clause concerning engagements outside Manchester, providing the Society had first call on his services, it decided that it would not be renewing his contract when it expired at the end of the 1932-33 season.

Matters came to a head early in 1933, while he was again on tour in the United States. The Hallé executive was naturally worried about arrangements for the following season and began informal discussions with other organizations. No formal communication of its intentions reached Harty in America, but he had become increasingly aware of the situation and also of the hostility, as he saw it, of certain members of the Committee, which had been simmering since the success of his own concert series in London. On 5 February, the date of his return to England, he forestalled any action by the committee by making a statement to the press announcing his resignation from the Hallé. It is clear that over the past few seasons major differences had grown up between Harty and the Hallé committee, and they could never be reconciled. His farewell concert took place on 23 March 1933 and in his speech he avoided any allusion to the events leading to his resignation. Instead he praised the qualities of the orchestra which he had conducted for the past thirteen years and finished by saying:

15. *Daily Express*, 24 March 1931.
16. Hubert Foss and Noel Goodwin, *London Symphony Orchestra* (London, 1954), 133-38.

45

The Hallé Years and After

> You honoured me greatly by handing over your orchestra to me, and as I hand it back
> to you I think I am not being immodest when I say I hand it back to you perhaps
> better than it was when I took it over. [17]

It was appropriate that in the summer of that year his achieve-
ments were recognized by the university of his own homeland, The
Queen's University of Belfast. Presenting him for an Honorary
Doctorate in Laws the Dean of the Faculty said:

> I commend to you Sir Hamilton Harty as a composer whose works are widely known;
> as a conductor, during several years, of one of the greatest orchestras in the kingdom;
> and, perhaps not least in our eyes, as a son of our own province, which rejoices in his
> brilliant career.

This was a fitting tribute, and one that formed a bond between
Harty and The Queen's University which was to be of the utmost
significance for the future.

* * *

Harty moved back to London and took up residence at 1 Norfolk
Road in St. John's Wood, a part of London he had known since he
had first come to England. His departure from the Hallé of course
marked the end of an important phase in his career, but in many
ways his musical activities continued as before. For example, there
was the constant schedule of recording sessions: he was musical
adviser to the Columbia Gramophone Company, who paid a
retaining fee for the sole rights in recording the Hallé Orchestra.
From 1924 to June 1933 all the orchestral works that he recorded
were with the Hallé (a few early ones were with an anonymous
'Symphony Orchestra', undoubtedly consisting of Hallé players). He
continued recording for Columbia after 1933, but now with the LSO
or the newly-formed London Philharmonic Orchestra. From
December 1935 he recorded for Decca.

Apart from recordings, his plans for the 1933-34 season were well
formulated when he moved to London, and included eight of the ten
LSO concerts and two important tours. The first of these was a fourth

17. Quoted in Kennedy, *op cit*, 241-42.

46

visit to America, in January and February 1934, where he conducted the Chicago Symphony Orchestra and the Rochester Philharmonic as he had done on previous visits. In April he embarked for Australia where he had been engaged by the Australian Broadcasting Commission for the months of May and June. The purpose of this much-publicized tour was to give a boost to the quality and prestige of orchestral playing in Australia. His peculiar gift for quickly getting to know his players and welding them into an efficient unit was of immense value, and the results he obtained with the ABC Symphony Orchestra earned him wide acclaim:

As guest conductor he might easily have contented himself with the comparatively humble objective of reforming the technical standard of orchestral playing in Australia. That the quality of the work heard last night represented a sensational advance upon previous performances by the same players was apparent to the most untrained listener. This reformation was not, however, brought about solely by pruning of errors, or even by the more positive method of inculcating technical virtues, but by the triple forces of faith, courtesy and imagination.[18]

During a visit to Sydney University as a guest of the Vice-Chancellor Harty heard an impromptu recital on the War Memorial Carillon, and promised to write a short piece for it on his return to London. The result was the Little Fantasy and Fugue which received its first public performance in Sydney on Christmas Day 1934. From Australia Harty sailed to Los Angeles where he was to conduct at the Hollywood Bowl in July, and in mid-August he travelled to Chicago for several concerts connected with the World Fair. Wherever he appeared he was enthusiastically greeted by the public and highly acclaimed by the critics — some of whom referred to him as 'the Irish Toscanini'.

Back home, on 22 November he received the highest honour in British Music, the Gold Medal of the Royal Philharmonic Society. The presentation was made by a fellow Ulsterman, the Marquis of Londonderry, during the interval of one of the Society's concerts in which Harty conducted (appropriately) Berlioz's overture 'Beatrice and Benedict', three movements from Mozart's Divertimento no.17, Brahms's Fourth Symphony, and his own Violin Concerto (played by

18. *Melbourne Argus*, 31 May 1934.

The Hallé Years and After

Paul Beard). Writing about this occasion, Constant Lambert said:

It is impossible to think of anyone more deserving this great honour than Sir Hamilton Harty. Fame has come to him later than to some men, but his name stands all the more solidly because he has never sought the cheap and evanescent rewards of fashion. Unlike many famous conductors Sir Hamilton is a musician first and foremost. We never feel that he is using a piece of music as a vehicle for his own virtuosity; on the contrary, he draws attention not to himself but to the composer, and that surely is the highest degree of the conductor's art.[19]

Although he continued to conduct the LSO concerts during 1934, his relationship with the Directors became increasingly uneasy. Following his long association with the Hallé, over which he had always exercised complete autonomy, he found it difficult to adjust to the self-governing régime of the LSO, whose Directors continued to reserve to themselves the right to engage a certain number of deputies each year, which Harty considered totally incompatible with the highest standards of performance. It became evident both to himself and the Directors that in such circumstances it would be impossible for him to work successfully, on anything of the nature of a permanent basis, with an orchestra so constituted, and so it was agreed that his contract with the LSO should be terminated, leaving him free to extend his European and American interests, and the Directors to revert to their original practice of engaging a series of guest conductors, which was perhaps better suited to their constitution.

In January and February 1935 he was once again in America, conducting in Chicago and Rochester. But the most notable musical event occurred towards the end of that year, on 6 November, when he conducted the first complete performance of William Walton's First Symphony.[20] Harty, who had been an admirer of Walton's music for some time,[21] said of the work: 'It was an enormous achievement for the composer ... and the English people ought to be very proud of this young man; his future will be of such tremendous

19. *Sunday Referee*, 25 November 1934.
20. He had previously conducted two performances of the incomplete work: see p. 80.
21. In an interview during his Australian tour he had singled out Walton and Constant Lambert as British composers he particularly admired (*Perth News*, 1 May 1934).

interest to all who love music.'[22] He later recorded the work with the London Symphony Orchestra for Decca. This première was shortly followed by another (21 November), that of Arnold Bax's Sixth Symphony, in a 'glowing and supremely effective performance'.[23] If the critics were somewhat equivocal about the new work Bax himself was ecstatic about the performance, writing to Harty:

> You realised everything I wanted and indeed took some of it into a world of beauty I did not know the work compassed. I am only afraid that no-one (except maybe yourself) will ever recreate tonight's experience for me. I am sure it was the best first performance any work ever had.

Following another American trip early in 1936 (during which he received an Honorary Doctorate from De Paul University, Chicago) he gave one of the most spectacular concerts of his career: on 4 March he conducted the BBC Symphony Orchestra and Choral Society, augmented to 450 performers, in a programme consisting of Berlioz's 'Grande messe des morts' and 'Symphonie funèbre et triomphale'. Earlier that week (2 March) he had prefaced the concert with a broadcast talk on the composer. Although the interminable arguments about the quality and stature of Berlioz continued to rage, there was no disputing that the concert was a magnificent and imposing occasion, 'a triumph for Harty and the composer for whom he has worked so hard and done so much'.[24]

22. *News Chronicle*, 7 November 1935.
23. William McNaught, *Evening News*, 22 November 1935.
24. J. A. Forsyth, *The Star*, 5 March 1936.

Memorial to William Harty (photo Linda Salem)

IV   LAST YEARS

John Barry

When the 1936 season had ended the bags were packed for Ireland.[1] In a sense Harty had never left Ireland: it was always at the back of his mind, and over the years he frequently returned for a summer break and occasionally made a brief visit to Hillsborough. He would drop in on the old haunts in a reticent sort of way, for once he had achieved recognition in the big world outside he seemed to want none of it amongst his own folk. A mere glance at the old house and an unobtrusive call at the church were enough to still a persistent emotional need. In the church he would walk slowly through the silent nave as though marking out and measuring every tread until he came face to face with his father's memorial carved on an unpretentious marble square set in the wall in the choir near the arch of the sanctuary.

The old folk of Hillsborough say that he would stand awhile, motionless, his eyes fixed on the words and the musical notation of Handel's 'I know that my Redeemer liveth', as though waiting until they would stir the depths of memory. Then he would turn away, glance up at the organ loft and leave as slowly and deliberately as he had come. Once and only once things had been different. It was in June 1925, just after he had received his knighthood. He consented to give a recital on the Snetzler organ and today, fifty years after the event, the older people still talk about it. According to the local bards the parish church (absolute tee-total seating capacity 450) held for the grand occasion an audience of three thousand and 'they' say that extra manpower had to be recruited to work the old-fashioned hand-blower in order to ensure that the heavily committed organ would be adequately supplied with air. No doubt even yet the tale has a capacity for growth in the telling.

1. The author is indebted to Miss Olive Baguley, the late Lady Thomson, Mr James Moore, Mr Robert McBride and Mrs Dorothy B. Stevenson (*née* Forster) for much information in this chapter.

Hillsborough Church

Last Years

The 'real' Irish holiday however was an affair of something like six weeks, usually in May and June when the countryside would be ablaze with the golden yellow of the gorse and the fly on the water made the trout feed. He loved Donaghadee — shades of the days of childhood! — and the psychologist might find significance in the fact that the house he rented there, down near the seashore at the Old Warren, was called 'Tir-na-Nog' — 'the Land of the Ever-young'. Rostrevor on Carlingford Lough at the foot of the Mournes was a comparatively new discovery and its great attributes were a mild climate, a profusion of trees and an unhurried peacefulness. And then in sharp contrast there was the North Antrim coast with the Causeway headlands where one could walk for miles and miles on the cliff-tops with nothing to break the stillness but the sound of the sea and the cry of gulls swirling below in the immensity of space. For fishing the best places (in addition to Scotland) were Lough Melvin and Lough Corrib in the West. He went there so often that the gillies watched for his coming with all the eagerness of thirsty men who knew they could be sure that 'Sir Hamilton' would invariably end the day with an invitation to 'split a bottle'. He had a standing order for a boat in any one of a dozen places and kept an outboard engine greased and stored and ready for use. But here again the psychologists might start looking for answers because somewhere about 1929 he stopped fishing — just stopped — cancelled the boats and gave his rods and outboard to his gillies at Lough Melvin. As far as can be discovered he never said a word of explanation to any of the friends with whom he long had been accustomed to share the once favourite pastime.

But fish or no fish, the passion for the Irish coast remained, and in the summer of 1936 the destination was Portballintrae near the Giant's Causeway. The June weather was ideal for walking and the thought of it brought a particular keenness of anticipation because of late he had been far from well. At the end of the hard 1935-6 season (spent mainly in the United States) he felt unaccountably tired. His usually sharp-edged concentration flagged. Even the smallest exertion was a bore. And his associates who were so familiar with his committed perfectionism were concerned to notice that suddenly he no longer seemed to care if a performance succeeded or failed. Des-

pite these things, however, Harty was cheerfully determined. He
insisted that a breath of Irish air was all that he needed. He would be
a new man in a month and return as fit as a fiddle to face the European tour planned for the autumn. Besides, a spell in the quietness
of the countryside would give him just the chance he sought to get
down to orchestral transcriptions of works of Chopin. This was a
thing his publishers had been pressing him to do since his success
with the 'Royal Fireworks' and 'Water Music' of Handel. He would
hire a piano and have it put into his room in the hotel at Portballintrae. His close friends, however, did not share his optimism. They
were sure that something was seriously amiss. And out of this conviction they encouraged his departure for Ireland at the earliest suitable
date because they knew that in Ireland the help so desperately
needed might be found.

It is a strange and touching part of the story that at this moment
of distress the person to whom the narrative turns should be Harty's
childhood companion, William Thomson of Annahilt. Now he was
Sir William Thomson, Professor of Medicine in Queen's University,
and acknowledged to be one of the most distinguished doctors of his
generation. In the way in which such things sometimes happen the
affection and trust of youth had not only remained unimpaired in
Harty and Thomson but had grown deeper throughout the years,
despite the fact that their professional achievements in adult life had
apparently taken them so far apart. Once Thomson had been made
aware of the anxiety being felt for his old friend he made a pretext
for visiting him at Portballintrae. It was immediately obvious to him
that he was dealing with a sick man. But the nature of the illness
could not be discerned and matters were complicated because the
change of air had already made Harty feel better — so much so that
he could scarcely remember that he had been so woe-begone a short
time before. Now he was certain (he said) that he was just being lazy
— lazy for the first time in years, and he intended to enjoy every
minute of it.

This exuberant mood was helped along by a meeting with a
kindred spirit, a young Ulsterman named James Moore who lived in
the nearby town of Bushmills. Moore was feeling his way towards a
career as an organist and music teacher (in which he was to make a

considerable name for himself in Ireland in the next thirty years) and he and Harty discovered that they shared an interest in Irish songs and folklore. Moore could sing (as well as play) and often the two men spent the evening hours in the hotel drawing room while 'Jimmy' gave a recital for his loudly-approving host who, with all his accustomed brilliance (Chopin forgotten), improvised an accompaniment on the hotel's notably inadequate piano.

Joy (as the saying is) was unconfined when Eric DeLamarter, conductor of the Chicago Symphony Orchestra, arrived unexpectedly — and an intended few hours visit stretched into a week. Anyone lucky enough to be around at the time — and knowledgeable enough to know 'who was who' — would have been given something on which to dine out for years if he had met James Moore's dilapidated car on the narrow road of an afternoon, Harty and DeLamarter crammed into the back seat, and all singing 'Phil the Fluter' or 'Slattery's Mounted Fut'. Incidentally, Harty and DeLamarter were old friends and about this time they were in fact discussing the possibility of an exciting partnership. The idea was that by and by they would both 'retire', pool their resources and found an Irish national orchestra based on a school of music in Queen's University, Belfast. Nor was this merely an idle dream because Harty had already gone so far as to open preliminary conversations on the proposal with government representatives in Ireland. The two men believed firmly that it could be done and their shared enthusiasm added a special zest to the fun and the songs in the long days of this Irish summer.

But there was nonetheless a sombre undercurrent to the happiness. The truth was that the hoped-for betterment in Harty's condition did not come about. He stayed on in Ireland until a return to London could be put off no longer. And then followed days of futility as he struggled to achieve the degree of concentration needed for the work of preparation for a European tour. It would not come. By the end of October his persistent assurance that he would be 'all right on the day' had to be acknowledged even by him to have worn pitifully thin. Thomson was called on again. He travelled to London and after a brief examination insisted that the tour at least should be cancelled and that Harty should come to him in Belfast for a thorough clinical investigation. Reluctantly Harty agreed. He was preoccupied mainly with regret that his withdrawal would bring disappointment and financial loss to other people. He had no thought (nor apparently had Sir William Thomson at this time) that his illness was other than trivial or that some simple treatment would not put things right. He wrote light-heartedly from Sir William and Lady Thomson's home in University Square giving humorous descriptions of the constant succession of specialists who came to prod and poke and emphasizing his confidence that 'the end of it all will be satisfactory'.

Thomson was painstakingly gentle and encouraging — encouraging even when the truth had been uncovered to his profound and lasting grief. This was not a simple case of overwork or nervous exhaustion. There was a deep-seated malignant growth in the right antrum of the brain, and the only hope lay in long courses of treatment to be arranged through the Radium Institute. Nothing else could be done. It was agreed by all who were in Thomson's confidence that if it were possible Harty must never know the full facts.

Surprisingly perhaps there were signs of improvement, despite surgery which had become necessary shortly after the treatment began and resulted in his right eye being removed. He spent some time in London and by the latter half of 1937 he was well enough to spend a few weeks in Rostrevor. In the following July and August there was a voyage to Jamaica. He loved the lazy days at sea and the warm sun of the Carribean. It all seemed to have worked a miracle and by the time he got back to London he had his manuscript paper out on the desk again and was determined to make a fresh start through the hard mental discipline of composition. Since the mid-1920s he had written little apart from several transcriptions of works by Handel and a revision of Schumann's Symphony in D minor. But now, in 1938, he produced settings of five Irish songs — 'The Fiddler of Dooney' by W. B. Yeats, 'At Easter' by Helen Lanyon, 'The Sailor Man' and 'Denny's Daughter' by Moira O'Neill and 'A Mayo Love Song' by Alice Milligan.

About this time too he started work on what was to be his last original composition, a tone-poem for soprano and orchestra entitled 'The Children of Lir'. The inspiration for 'Lir' had come two years before on his fateful holiday at Portballintrae. One afternoon James Moore had taken him for a walk that led them along the stretch of

'Finola': bas-relief by Rosamond Praeger (photo D. A. C. Gould)

the Blackrock Strand, over the rocks at Runkerry, and up the hill to the quaint little school which had been erected by the family of the local 'big house' as a memorial to their father, Lord Macnaghten. The Macnaghtens had commissioned the sculptress Rosamond Praeger to come to this out-of-the-way place and carve an appropriate adornment for the entrance hall. And there it was — in *bas-relief* — 'The Children of Lir'. As they stood there with the sea murmuring on the rocks below Harty heard again (for he had known it from his childhood) the strange tale of Finola and her three little brothers who were turned into swans, and doomed to swim for ever in the treacherous Sea of Moyle, unless perchance they heard the sound of a Christian bell. Centuries passed and a church was built above the cliff and a bell was rung. On the instant the curse was broken and the swans took human shape again — beautiful princes, children of the king. But at once reality laid hold of them. They grew old in the twinkling of an eye, and died.

Harty returned to London not merely with this story in his mind but also with the desolate beauty of the place troubling his spirit. It was all this which re-emerged when he took up his pen in an effort to exorcize his own misfortune at the time of his temporary recovery in 1938. Before the year was out he was well enough to accept an offer from the BBC to conduct two symphony concerts to be broadcast from the London studios on 23 December and 2 February 1939. These he regarded as trial runs for his first public appearance since the onset of his illness. This was to be on 1 March 1939 in the Queen's Hall and there he would conduct the first performance of 'The Children of Lir'. He would have the BBC Symphony Orchestra, and Isobel Baillie, to whom it would be a mark of affection after their long association since he had first 'discovered' her in Manchester in 1921. It was a great occasion. Harty was warmly received by a capacity audience. There certainly was no doubt about the warmth of the welcome which greeted him on his return to the rostrum; no doubt about the degree of goodwill which came to him from all sides. But in general there was a lack of enthusiasm amongst the critics for 'The Children of Lir'. Neville Cardus, however, seems to have understood better than some of the others:

Last Years

[Harty] was given a tumultuous and affectionate welcome from a crowded Queen's Hall. And he at once lifted the occasion far above sentiment and goodwill by conducting with simple mastery a magnificent performance of a new work of his own and one of the most poetic compositions of any British composer of the last decade or two.

His poem for orchestra, 'The Children of Lir', is an act of courage in these days when music is afraid not to sound obviously modern and when system is regarded as of more consequence than sensibility. Sir Hamilton trusts to the traditional stuff of his art, and by sincerity and the Irishman's gracious tenderness he has given us a work which appeals to the heart and moves us with beauty of tone and beauty of conception. [2]

It is unlikely, of course, that Cardus at the time could have known anything of the real truth of Harty's predicament. His understanding was therefore all the more remarkable when one considers with hindsight that 'The Children of Lir' can be seen to have a deeply personal content. Taking into account all the circumstances of the time it can be discerned that this was not only Harty's last piece of creative writing but the one which above all others may represent a *cri de coeur*. Is there an autobiographical overtone in the words which Harty himself used in his programme note for the first performance to summarize the plight and the nobility of spirit of the Children of Lir?

The introduction, *Lento e con dignità*, illustrates the thoughts of one who stands on the Antrim cliffs on a day of storm and tempest, and recalls the sorrowful story of the enchanted Children of Lir while gazing down on the turbulent Sea of Moyle — a picture of heaving waters, clouds of spray, and screaming seagulls. In imagination he sees these four children in all their grace and dignity changed by an evil spell into the shape of swans, but facing their tragic future with bravery and defiance.

And he included then a quotation from an old song:

Silent, O Moyle, be the roar of thy water,
Break not, ye breezes, your chain of repose,
While, murmuring mournfully, Lir's only daughter,
Tells to the night-star her tale of woes.
When shall the swan, her death-note singing,
Sleep with wings in darkness furled?
When will heaven, its sweet bell ringing,
Call my spirit from this stormy world? [3]

2. *Manchester Guardian*, 2 March 1939.
3. From Thomas Moore's *Irish Melodies*. Esposito had set the melody for violin and piano in his *Irish Melodies*, op.56 (Dublin, 1903).

Last Years

Whether or not Harty had any conscious awareness of his plight, the fact that he should have chosen to concentrate so closely on this theme at this juncture in his life may have been deeply significant.

Summer came (1939) and apparent convalescence continued, helped by a cruise to the Azores and another stay at Rostrevor. By the autumn a large programme of engagements had been arranged to cover the coming months. In November he was back in the North of England (the first time since his illness) for a Liverpool Philharmonic concert which included the first performance of his 'John Field Suite', which he had recently completed. Cardus noted that Harty was less energetic in his gestures than of old, but that the increase in quiet supervision clearly meant more than physical adjustments; it meant also a strengthening and ripening of aesthetic outlook. Referring to the 'John Field Suite', Cardus concluded:

It was no mere transcription. The orchestration and general layout of Field's charming if naive rhythms and tunes were evidence of assimilation to another form and idiom.[4]

Three more Liverpool Philharmonic concerts followed and there were also several engagements with the BBC, which had recently left London to escape the bombings and were housed in the Colston Hall in Bristol.

The BBC's move was a sign of the times. In 1940 concert-giving was virtually in a state of suspense because of the war, and the air of hopelessness was accentuated for Harty by massive bomb-damage to his house in St. John's Wood. His music-room was littered with debris, the roof caved in, windows were gone and there was neither gas nor electricity. Obviously life there was no longer possible. Disconsolate, he left London and after monotonous searching and a month of make-do in an hotel he took a flat in Brunswick Square in Hove, where the front windows overlooked the sea and at night the sky was lighted by the flashing of search-lights and distant guns. Concert engagements now were few and far between, and even these were beyond the capability of a sick man. The nauseating courses of treatment had begun again — with the nearest available equipment under war-time restriction in a London hospital sixty miles away. He conducted for the last time with the BBC Symphony Orchestra at

4. *Manchester Guardian*, 9 November 1939.

60

Memorial Bird Bath

Last Years

Tunbridge Wells on 1 December 1940. Two months later he was dead.

In the preceding days he had seemed to regain something of his old spirit, and apparently he was still unaware of the true nature of his illness and ready to talk about plans of what he might do when summer would come. In the meantime, despite the cold, there was something to be said for the fading daylight of a winter's afternoon, a short walk down to the shore and then back again to the fireside and a cup of strong tea — like the tea Mrs Harty used to make on a frosty day when the children came running home from school. It seemed to be no more than a simple chill that sent him to bed on Monday 17 February 1941 and there was every hope that with warmth and a rest he would soon be well again. But septic pneumonia put him beyond all human aid, and two days later, at ten minutes to six in the evening, he died without the smallest pain. He was sixty-one years of age.

When the war had ended and unrestricted travel between England and Ireland again became possible his ashes were brought to Hillsborough. The burial place in the green-sward near the west door of the church is marked by a Bird Bath of Limerick limestone carved by Rosamond Praeger and bearing the inscription 'Hamilton Harty 1879-1941'.

There is a peaceful loneliness in this place where in summer the bees murmur in the linden trees and at Easter-tide the daffodils spread their glory all around. Little has changed since Bertie Harty walked along the leafy path on his way to the organ loft to sit and listen when his father filled the church with stupendous sound. Or since the days when he returned as a man with a world in his hand to stand silent in the shadows of the choir and read again his father's name, and the music of Handel — 'I know that my Redeemer liveth...'.

Little has changed indeed. So be it. Except of course that 'William' and 'Mrs Harty' and the ginger cat and all the joyful rest of the things have become part of the local lore, a tale to be told again and again. And the Hillsborough community has been enriched beyond measure by a story which to them records not only the great achievement of a child of the village but also the excep-

Memorial Plaque at Hillsborough, 1964

tional relationship of mutual love and sensitivity which held like a bond of steel between the gentle father and his prodigiously talented son.

Postlude

On 22 April 1964 a memorial plaque was unveiled by Miss Olive Baguley outside the house in Ballynahinch Street, Hillsborough, where Harty lived as a boy. Miss Baguley, for many years the Secretary of the Hallé Concerts Society, had severed her connection with the Society at the same time as Harty, in order to become his personal secretary, and effectively organize the business side of his life, which had by then assumed vastly increased dimensions. During his long illness, which necessitated prolonged and complicated courses of medical treatment, she nursed him as devotedly as she had worked for him; and after the war it was she who arranged for his ashes to be interred at Hillsborough. Following the announcement of his death many offers were received from conductors and musical organizations in England and America, anxious to acquire the contents of his music library, but remembering the hopes and intentions he had so often expressed of returning to Ireland to do something worthwhile for music in the province, she felt it would have been his wish that the complete collection should be presented to The Queen's University of Belfast, which in 1933 had conferred on him the Honorary Degree of LLD. When in 1951 it became necessary to consider how the royalties from his music could best be used, it was decided to create the Hamilton Harty Chair of Music at Queen's University, and in 1952 to institute an annual Hamilton Harty Memorial Concert at which one of his major works would be performed. In the same year a Travelling Scholarship (subsequently increased in number) bearing his name was established.[5]

In 1967 Miss Baguley commissioned a choir verge for Hillsborough

---

5. The debt of the university to Miss Baguley was acknowledged in 1960 when she was awarded an honorary degree of Master of Arts in recognition of 'the imaginative munificence [which has] ensured that Ulster shall keep in evergreen remembrance the name of one of her greatest sons'.

Choir Verge with Nightingale Motif

parish church, made from gold melted down from the many gifts Sir Hamilton received during his career. On the head of it, in blue enamel, is depicted a nightingale — a reference to one of his most notable works — and on the reverse there is the following inscription:

> We give Thee but Thine own,
> Whate'er the gift may be,
> For all we have is Thine alone,
> A trust, O Lord, from Thee.

On 16 October 1976 a plaque was erected by the Regency Society of Brighton and Hove, at 33 Brunswick Square, Hove, to mark the house in which Harty died. It was unveiled by David Greer, Professor of Music at The Queen's University of Belfast.

V MEMORIES OF SIR HAMILTON

Leonard Hirsch

My first meeting with Sir Hamilton Harty was in 1922, at the Hallé offices above Forsyth's music shop in Manchester. I was in my teens, and it was my first audition. Naturally, I was nervous and anxious to do my best, and not sure what to expect when I came face to face with such a distinguished conductor. I was shown into his room, and he immediately put me at my ease with a warm smile and a welcome I will never forget. He asked me what I would like to play, and I offered a choice of Lalo's 'Symphonie espagnole', the Max Bruch Concerto, or the Bach Chaconne. He chose the Bruch. All I can really remember of that audition is not how I played, but how wonderfully Harty accompanied me on the piano. Within a few days I received a letter from the Hallé secretary, saying Sir Hamilton was pleased to offer me a place in the first violins.

I will never forget my first rehearsals with Harty. I was the last first violin, but I felt that Harty was watching me most of the time. When I told the other players about this they replied, 'So do we all.' I soon learned to adjust my music stand in such a way that I could focus my eye on him, and not miss a movement. Few, if any, conductors could weave such a spell as he did over an orchestra. His vital personality made an enormous impression on all the players, and we could give a faultless performance after only one rehearsal. And not just the classics, but of new works as well. For me, as a young musician wanting to learn all I could, rehearsals were not only a lesson but a real pleasure. Few conductors could, without asking, so exactly indicate by the beat the kind of staccato, or the pulse of the vibrato, or the length of the note required. Harty never raised his voice, but he went to enormous pains to make sure everyone understood every detail of the musical value of the work. When things were not going right, he would stop and quietly explain what he wanted in such a way that it would be impossible not to get it right next time. Contrary to what is sometimes stated,[1] he liked uniform bowing provided it did not detract from the continuity of the music.

Rehearsals were not without their lighter moments, with Harty's flashes of wit. I remember one rehearsal when he kept on stressing to a certain brass player the need to play softer. The player repeated the passage, but Harty was still not satisfied, especially when the player pointed out 'But Sir Hamilton, it's marked *forte.*' Harty replied, 'Well, make it twenty!' Another time while we were rehearsing Berlioz's 'Romeo and Juliet', he suddenly stopped and tapped the stand. 'Boys', he said, 'remember you are making love to the girl, not dragging her round by the hair of her head!' During rehearsals, Sir Hamilton played through the music and then often went into the minutest detail with the players, discussing the shape of phrase, tonal quality, and especially the range of dynamics — expecting the softest *pianissimo* imaginable, and also the most thunderous *fortissimos* and climaxes. In a flash, he could whip up the orchestra to white-heat excitement.

His left-hand directions were an inspiration. I have heard conductors admit how terrified they have been to beat the opening bar of Strauss's 'Don Juan', wondering if the orchestra would get off the ground after the impact of the first beat. Often the philosophy has been, 'Give the beat and hope for the best.' But when Harty conducted the work, there was no doubt what was expected. His timing was so exact that the cascade of seven semiquavers that follow the downbeat sounded like a tornado. When Strauss himself conducted the Hallé at one of the Saturday series known as the Brand Lane Concerts, naturally the programme included one of his own compositions. When he announced we would begin the rehearsal with 'Don Juan', we all wondered what changes Strauss would make to Harty's interpretation of his work. However, to our amazement we played the work straight through without a stop. Strauss made few gestures — his beat was small. At the end of the work, he said 'Thank you, gentlemen. I shall not forget your wonderful playing. There is nothing I wish to alter. Let us now continue the rehearsal

1. See, for example, John F. Russell, 'Hamilton Harty', *Music & Letters*, xxii (1941), 216-24; and Michael Kennedy, *The Hallé Tradition* (Manchester, 1960), 214.

with Mozart's G Minor Symphony.'

During his rehearsal explanations to players, I never once heard Harty try to sing or hum a phrase. It may be that he had no singing voice. But what he could do, in his own inimitable way, was to whistle it, most beautifully, with perfect intonation and pitch. It was something to see and hear — a great conductor whistling his way through a difficult passage.

There was a rather uncomfortable experience one day, when the orchestral parts for 'Omar Khayyám', the massive work for soloists, chorus and orchestra by Bantock, failed to arrive in time for the performance. To everyone's astonishment, Sir Hamilton saved the day by condensing the score, and without any notice, played the whole work on the piano, to the amazement of the whole orchestra who remained on the platform throughout the performance.

As an accompanist, either with the orchestra or at the piano, Harty stood alone: it was uncanny, the way he could anticipate the intentions of the soloist. Sometimes the performers would stretch the music beyond the limits of artistic licence, but Harty was always with them. So much so that on one memorable occasion, when Schnabel was playing Brahms's Second Piano Concerto with the orchestra, Harty spotted a memory slip when Schnabel skipped two bars in the last movement. Immediately, Sir Hamilton adjusted the mistake, indicated to the players what had happened, and the performance went on without a hitch. In the ante-room after the concert, Schnabel was in a very happy mood, and he told Harty how much he had enjoyed playing with the orchestra. 'Do you know,' said Schnabel, 'the Hallé Orchestra is almost as good as the Berlin Philharmonic.' 'Do you really think so,' replied Harty, 'I think they are even two bars better!' Years later, I asked Schnabel if he remembered the time when he played the Brahms in Manchester, with Sir Hamilton conducting. He replied, 'Shall I ever forget it — and the two bars I owed Sir Hamilton. Never, but never, in my whole life have I ever experienced such a magnificent accompaniment.'

Schnabel was just one star in a brilliant galaxy of soloists who came to Manchester during the years that Harty was with the Hallé, including pianists like Backhaus, Busoni, Cortot, Dohnányi, Gieseking, Godowsky, Hambourg, Haskil, Hess, Hofmann,

69

Horowitz, Moiseiwitsch, Pouishnoff, Rakhmaninov, Rosenthal, Rubinstein, Siloti, and Solomon. Backhaus had so much admiration for Harty that he said to me, 'If only I could afford to engage the Hallé Orchestra with Sir Hamilton Harty to accompany me at every concert — that would be my greatest wish.' Another pianist, who had better remain nameless, kept popping up from the piano during rehearsal to indicate certain things in the score to Harty. The great man did not react too well to this constant interference. To the orchestra's amusement, eventually Harty said, 'Suppose *you* conduct, and I'll play the piano!' The orchestra knew full well that Harty *could* play the concerto, but the pianist certainly could not conduct it.

To continue the list of soloists eager to share the platform with Harty were violinists such as Jelly d'Aranyi, Brodsky (my teacher), Catterall, Elman, Heifetz, Hubermann, Menges, Sammons, Szigeti, Thibaud and Ysaÿe. The cellists included Casals, Cassadó and Suggia, and the great viola players William Primrose and Lionel Tertis also appeared.

Singers who came to Manchester included Stiles Allen, Norman Allin, Astra Desmond, Cesare Formichi, Plunket Greene, Roy Henderson, Heddle Nash, Agnes Nicholls, Maggie Teyte and Eva Turner. Isobel Baillie imprinted herself on the hearts of the audience with her rendering of the soprano solos in 'Messiah'. So did the Australian soprano Florence Austral with her magnificent interpretation of the last act of 'Götterdämmerung', her voice soaring above the orchestra.

By the late 1920s, I was promoted to principal second violin, and had the opportunity of playing in a number of chamber music concerts conducted by Harty. One of these was at the Royal Dublin Society (known by concert-goers as the RDS). The soloist was Commendatore Michele Esposito and Sir Hamilton often spoke of his indebtedness to him for advice and encouragement. Esposito played a Mozart concerto on this occasion, and during the performance it was obvious what a bond existed between teacher and pupil. Harty was so humble and affectionate in the presence of his former professor.

The following day, we had another treat in store — we were to give a concert at Woodbrook, the home of Sir Stanley Cochrane, about ten miles outside Dublin. Harty had a surprise up his sleeve for us, but he did not reveal it until we arrived at the house: there to greet us was the famous Count John McCormack. The mansion house at Woodbrook provided a magnificent setting for that evening's concert, at which John McCormack sang with the orchestra. He also sang a group of solos, accompanied on the piano by Harty — the kind of accompaniment singers must dream of, but rarely get. McCormack's voice was pure music, his diction perfect. It was a marvellous evening.

During his tours of America in the 1930s Harty made a tremendous impact, and he had many triumphs. Every time he conducted the Chicago Symphony Orchestra he was greeted with a fanfare — a tribute normally accorded only on the very rarest of occasions.

It would be impossible to write about Harty the conductor without mentioning his great love for the music of Berlioz. To me, no one could ever approach Harty's masterly interpretation of the Fantastic Symphony. Harty conveyed to our senses through the medium of sound all the superabundance of feeling and tenderness. At the very opening of the work members of the orchestra had a very strange, inner feeling that, somewhere around them, was the presence of the great composer himself. I thought it was just my own imagination, but this eerie feeling was later confirmed by many other players. Harty had such an incredible insight into the composer's mind, that he seemed to be re-creating the very spirit of Berlioz before us. Berlioz was far from fashionable at that time, but largely through Harty, his works came back into the repertoire of many great orchestras. During the 1930-31 series of 'Hamilton Harty Symphony Concerts' in London, the concert on 6 February contained the Fantastic Symphony. Here are some of the reviews:

...the playing of the Hallé Orchestra was a sustained joy from beginning to end. It was a real demonstration of discipline, plus enthusiasm — qualities, of course, that cannot exist without the right sort of conductor. (*Daily Telegraph*, 7 February)

The most obstinate detractor of Berlioz had to admit the charm and persuasiveness of Sir Hamilton's advocacy, even if he reserved the opinion that after a concerto by Brahms the symphony sounded like the music of a clever and unbalanced child. (*Glasgow Herald*)

Memories of Sir Hamilton

A large audience heard a magnificent performance of Berlioz 'Symphonie Fantastique' — in which there was much more fire and life than in a recent performance of the work under Dr. Mengelberg. But then, who understands Berlioz as Sir Hamilton Harty does? (*Daily Dispatch*)

Berlioz's Fantastic Symphony gave us the finest orchestral playing heard in London for a long time. (*Daily News & Chronicle*)

I have never heard some parts better played: the strings *sang* the 'idée fixe' motive, for example, like a single singer of genius, while the suggestion, at more than one point, of foreground and background in the simultaneous handling of this theme and that of the ball was a subtlety beyond praise. (Ernest Newman, *Sunday Times*, 8 February)

It really is a great pity that Harty never recorded the Fantastic Symphony. Fortunately, some of his other Berlioz recordings were re-issued in 1971.[2]

Harty was genuinely concerned about the members of his orchestra, especially the ones he particularly respected. Often he entertained groups of players, and on one occasion, after an excellent meal, it was suggested that we play poker. Unfortunately, I lost. But as we left, Harty patted me on the shoulder and said with a smile 'What's lost to a friend is not lost!' In fact he excelled at poker, and I have been told that it almost had to be written into Moiseiwitsch's contract that whenever he came to the Hallé, Sir Hamilton should give him a game after the concert — and that Harty invariably won.

Harty was known by name throughout the North, and not only by music-lovers. On one occasion, when Sir Thomas Beecham was in Manchester, he asked the receptionist at the Midland Hotel for his usual suite. He was told it was already booked. Beecham replied, 'Do you know who I am? I am Sir Thomas Beecham, and I must have the apartment.' The receptionist countered, 'I don't care if you are Sir Hamilton Harty. You can't have it this time.'

In the field of opera Beecham was such a towering figure that other operatic ventures tended to wilt under his shadow. Referring to the demise of one such venture, the British National Opera

2. World Record Club, SH 148. For reviews of it see Basil Ashmore in *Hi-Fi News*, July 1971, and Robert Layton in *The Gramophone*, August 1971.

Company in 1929, Harty said 'British Opera is dying — slowly but surely dying — of T.B.'[3]

Another example of Harty's gentle but penetrating humour came after a performance of the Tchaikovsky Violin Concerto by a young player making his début with the Hallé. I thought that, although his tone was rather thin, he played beautifully. Afterwards I told Sir Hamilton how much I had enjoyed the performance. Without hesitation, he said to me, 'Have you ever looked through binoculars the wrong way. That's how it seemed to me.'

Sir Hamilton's retirement from the Hallé came as a great shock to the orchestra and music-lovers throughout the North. During his thirteen years reign in Manchester he had made the Hallé one of the best disciplined, most artistic and most adventurous orchestras in the world. I was there, of course, for his last concert, the Pension Fund Concert, and there were scenes of wild enthusiasm. Harty was given an uproarious welcome, and loudly applauded at the end of each work. After the interval, he made a valedictory speech in which he outlined his work with the Hallé. 'All orchestras have their own characteristics,' he said. 'The chief characteristics of your own orchestra are sincerity and power of passionate expression. There is also a rather dark and sombre and, one might say, almost tragic colour, especially in the strings. I found this when I came here, and it was owing to my great predecessor Hans Richter. Those qualities are characteristic of the North rather than of any other part of the country. I have tried to preserve these qualities in the orchestra.'

Sir Hamilton spoke with special feeling about his 'ties' with the orchestra. There was one tie in particular — 'My relations with the members of the orchestra,' he said, fingering his neckwear, 'may be judged from the fact that I am wearing at this moment a tie borrowed from one of the first violins.' He went on more seriously, 'The members of this orchestra are the dearest friends of mine — the most valuable friends I have ever had, and I shall never have better. I am grateful. They reserve nothing when playing great music, and it almost seems to me sometimes as though they were prepared to give the very soul out of their bodies if necessary. In fact, when they are

3. Neville Cardus, *Sir Thomas Beecham* (London, 1961), 97.

73

playing great music, I think that is what they really do.'

After saying goodbye in English, he then said goodbye in Irish — with his Irish Symphony. At the end of this brilliant performance, with the applause thundering round the hall, he bowed his thanks and shook hands warmly with many of us. The audience was standing, the noise deafening. But Harty held up his hand for silence, and told them, 'Do something that will please me enormously. Applaud the orchestra.' It was a typical and sincere gesture.

VI 'DEAR SIR HAMILTON': LETTERS 1915-41

David Greer

The contrast between the public face and the private world of great men is a subject of endless fascination to novelists and students of human nature, and one always looks to their correspondence for insights into their lives and characters which would not otherwise be apparent. It is a mistake, however, to regard the public image as not quite real: how a man presents himself before the public gives just as true a picture of some aspect of him (for better or worse) as any private letter. In the case of Harty the letters show a remarkable consistency in the picture they give of him, consistent with each other and with the popular image of him, and if any contradictions are to be found they are no more than the contradictions which are present in us all.

Most of Harty's correspondence was destroyed when his St. John's Wood home was bombed in 1940, but a fair quantity still remains. The letters quoted or mentioned in this chapter are ones received by him, and so we see him in the manner in which others addressed themselves to him. But they are also illuminating on many aspects of musical life in the first half of the century.[1] The earliest surviving letter is one from the author J. B. Fagan, dated 1 June 1915, concerning the music for 'The Singer of Shiraz'. The most interesting thing that we learn from it is that Harty was to receive £100 *for every performance*, which was very generous payment for those days. But Harty's correspondence really began to grow in quantity from 1920, when he took over conductorship of the Hallé and became increasingly involved in its administration. Soon after his appointment he wrote to Elgar asking if any new work was forthcoming. The reply came on black-edged paper (Elgar's wife had died in March 1920)

---

1. All quotations from the letters preserve the original spelling, punctuation and capitals. However, the date and place of origin have been regularized.

and it strikes a rather sour note:

Hampstead, 18 April 1921

Dear Mr Hamilton Harty:
    No: there is no thought of a new work. It is very good of you to suggest Manchester
— but I should think the good people there wd be more surprised than pleased if you
produced a new work of mine.

Kind regards
Yours sincerely
Edward Elgar

In the years which followed, however, Harty gave some eloquent performances of Elgar's music which the composer acknowledged. In a
letter dated 4 March 1926 he thanked Harty warmly for a performance of 'The Dream of Gerontius' and he continued in this
friendly vein a few days later (9 March). A puzzling feature of this
second letter is the postscript:

P.S. I fear your surmise regarding the 'Enigma' is too remote to be encouraged: I will
leave you the solution in my will!
Forgive me if I call to your notice the bar before 193 (Apostles) — in a fit of laziness I
suppose, I wrote one bar — it should have been *four*; — you will see the *great cresc.* &
the *fff* tearing of the 3 Trumpets

Harty must have mentioned that he was doing 'The Apostles' (he
recorded an extract soon afterwards), but Elgar's reference to 'the bar
before 193' does not accord with anything in the printed scores. By
this time Harty felt confident enough to mention once more the
question of a new work, and Elgar's response was slightly less bleak
than previously: 'I fear there is [not] much chance of anything new
for some time to come: when the things (or thing) I am engaged
upon are presentable I will of course let you know at the earliest.' (23
March 1926)
    Since 1924 Elgar had been Master of the King's Musick, and we
get a glimpse of the more humdrum administrative chores that the
honour entailed (along with the composition of festive odes and
marches) in two letters dated 1929. Under the impressive letter-head
appropriate to that position we read:

76

'Dear Sir Hamilton': Letters 1915-41

My dear Harty,

Urgent.

Private and confidential.

I understand that Princess Mary will be pleased to go to one of your concerts and is thinking of choosing the 13th. December. Let me have the programme for that date at once (I left mine at the Palace) and tell me if you have already any Patronage, etc. We must not clash with anything: please do not mention the matter until confirmed.

Kind regards,

Yours sincerely,

Edward Elgar

P.S. I am asked "how many seats would be placed at Princess Mary's disposal". Telephone Stratford on Avon 30.

P.S. — I shall be in tomorrow morning (Friday) till 10.30 a.m. perhaps you can ring me up — as early as you like.

The concert in question was one of the 1929-30 series of 'Hamilton Harty Symphony Concerts'. The rather flustered tone of the postscripts tells its own story and clearly the matter was not laid to rest there and then, for a little later another letter arrived in Elgar's terrible scrawl (though for illegibility the prize must go to Plunket Greene):

Worcester, 7 December 1929

My dear Harty: I understand that the princess *is* going to the concert: as I asked that 'requirements' should be sent on I shall probably not hear further: I am sorry there seems to have been some indecision but I trust all will be well.

Best regards

Yours sincerely,

Edward Elgar

After all this it is pleasant to report that all seems to have gone well on the night. A letter dated 21 December to Elgar from Sybil Kenyon-Slaney (Lady in Waiting) asks him to tell Harty that the Princess wished him to know how much she and her guests had enjoyed the occasion. The last letter Harty received from Elgar was written just two months before the composer died.

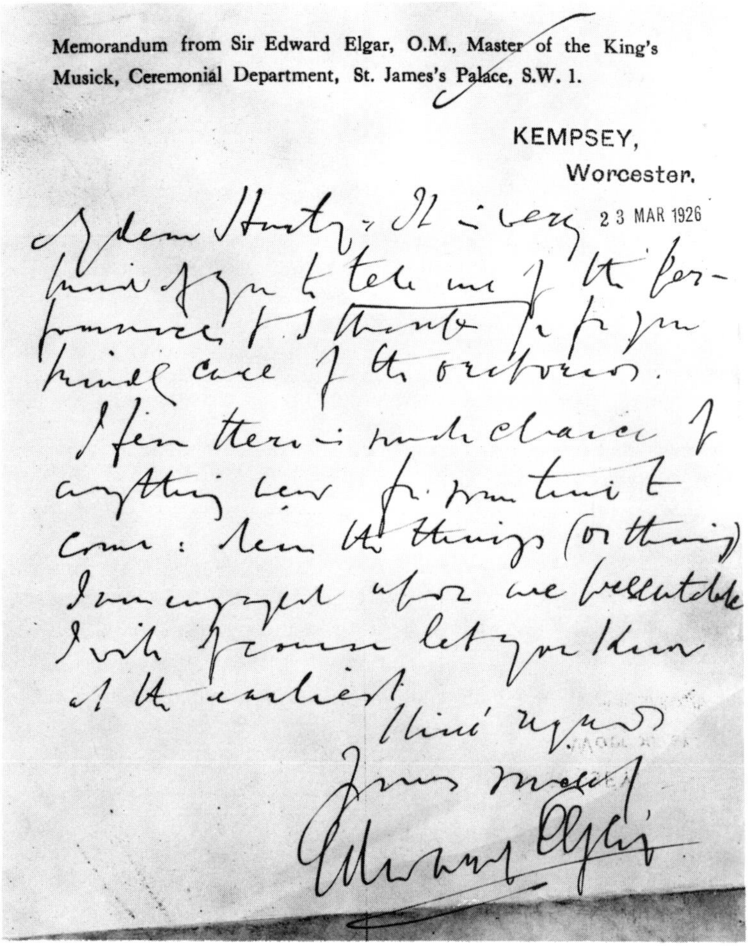

Memorandum from Sir Edward Elgar, O.M., Master of the King's Musick, Ceremonial Department, St. James's Palace, S.W. 1.

KEMPSEY,
Worcester.

23 MAR 1926

My dear Hartley: It is very kind of you to tell me of the performance & I thank you for your kind care of the orchestra.

I fear there is small chance of anything new for some time to come: even the things (or thing) I am engaged upon are unsettled. I will of course let you know at the earliest.

Kind regards
Yours sincy
Edward Elgar

Letter from Sir Edward Elgar, 23 March 1926

'Dear Sir Hamilton': Letters 1915-41

Nursing Home, Worcester, 19 December 1933

Dictated

My dear Harty,

Your very welcome letter reached me still in the nursing home. It is very cheering to receive such a warm tribute from so great a man as yourself. Nothing could give me greater pleasure than to hear that you take such a real interest in my music.

I heard that your performance of the A flat symphony was fine and I am very grateful to you for all your kind care of it.

With all good wishes and kindest regards. Believe me to be

Yours ever sincerely,
signed Edward Elgar

All in all, the handful of letters from Elgar makes rather sad reading. Spanning the period from his wife's death to his own last days they come from a man disconsolate and out-of-tune with the times to one who was at the peak of his fame and fortune, and the stilted compliments betray rather than disguise the lack of zest for life. In this respect they make a striking contrast with the letters of Delius and his wife Jelka — as different as 'Gerontius' is from 'A Mass of Life'. Though Delius had to live with terrible physical suffering, and his wife live with its consequences, their letters are full of genuine spirit and interest. Whereas Elgar almost invariably regrets that he was not actually able to hear a particular performance, Delius *listened*, even though it meant picking up a performance in Manchester on a crackly wireless in his retreat at Grez-sur-Loing. The following letters convey something of this *esprit* as well as giving us a glimpse of life in the Delius home.

Grez-sur-Loing, 26 February 1932

Dear Sir Hamilton,

To-day I am sending you a dictated letter from my husband and a photograph, taken just before his birthday, and which — I hope — you will receive safely.

Delius looked just like that so rapt and happy during the memorable performance of the Mass of Life, from time to time remarking on some special beauty of the rendering. We both enjoyed it immensely, as well as the beautiful performance of "Life's Dance" last night. Those are the glorious moments that lift us over many rather drab times.

79

'Dear Sir Hamilton': Letters 1915-41

I am so glad that the Northern Regional comes through to us so well. Yesterday there was no fading and your Violin Concerto sounded splendid.

It is my lot to manage the wireless set and I am always terribly anxious that any catastrophe might happen; as Delius is *so* keen to listen and enjoys it more than anything else when he can listen to such exquisite performances.

Sincerely yours
Jelka Delius

Grez-sur-Loing, 26 February 1932

Dear Harty,

Your kind and sympathetic letter gave me the greatest pleasure. Only one who felt and understood my music entirely could have given such a performance as you did.

And last night, I listened in again to Northern Regional, and you gave again the best performance of "Life's Dance" that I have yet heard. (And I have heard it often in Germany.)

I heard your concerto also for the first time and it seemed to me superbly played by Mr. Barker. After a first hearing the first movement especially appealed to me with its touchingly beautiful second subject.

I hope I shall soon have the opportunity of hearing it again. I like Constant Lambert's "Rio Grande". I think he is the most gifted of the young lot. He has got something to say.

Your grateful friend
Frederick Delius

One of the most interesting letters in the Harty archives is one written by William Walton during the composition of his First Symphony. Walton began work on this in 1932 while Harty was still with the Hallé: contrary to what has been stated elsewhere[2] the first performance was not promised to the Hallé, though the work *was* composed for Harty. A letter from the composer to Miss Olive Baguley dated 14 April 1962 makes this quite clear: 'I can confirm that my first Symphony was composed for Sir Hamilton *personally* & for no specific orchestra & that he was free to give the first performance with whatever orchestra he thought fit.' As is well known, the composition of the finale gave Walton much trouble, so much so that the symphony was first performed without the finale by Harty

2. Michael Kennedy, *The Hallé Tradition* (Manchester, 1960), 274.

and the London Symphony Orchestra on 3 December 1934, and again the following April. The first complete performance was given by Harty and the BBC Symphony Orchestra on 6 November 1935. The work had been announced for two years running in the prospectus of the LSO before it was completed, and no doubt this embarrassing situation was the main reason for the decision to perform it incomplete, a decision in which Harty undoubtedly played an important part. As Hugh Ottaway has observed,[3] the incomplete performance and the attendant publicity generated intense interest in the work which contributed to the spectacular success of its first complete performance. On the other hand, the common knowledge that Walton had had trouble in solving the 'problem' of the finale made listeners particularly sensitive to that movement, and the critical opinion that he did not quite find the 'right' solution has dogged the work ever since. The undated letter to Harty bears out the suggestion that the problem was as much an emotional one as a technical one: the mood of profound melancholy which found expression in the Adagio prevented him from proceeding straight on to the finale.

Ascona, [no date]

Dear Sir Hamilton,
   Thank you so much for your letter.
   I'm sorry that I've been so slow in producing my symphony, but actually I don't think it is any the worse for it, in fact, I hope & think, that it promises to be better than any work I've written hitherto, but that may be only an optimistic reaction to the months of despair I've been through, when I thought I should never be able to write another note. However the 1st movement is finished & the 2nd ought to be in another 10 days or so. But having dissapointed [sic] you once, I feel chary about fixing any date to its ultimate completion, but it ought to be ready sometime for next season.
   I must say, I think it almost hopeless for anyone to produce anything in any of the arts in these days. It is practically impossible to get away from the general feeling of hopelessness & chaos which exists everywhere, however one may try — so you mustn't think I'm an exception, & one capable of encompassing all difficulties — producing a masterpiece. But I'm trying my best.
   I am very grateful to you for taking so much interest in the work, & I really hope to produce something worthy of your genius as a conductor.

3. Hugh Ottaway, 'Walton's First Symphony', *The Musical Times*, cxiii (1972), 254, and cxiv (1973), 998.

'Dear Sir Hamilton': Letters 1915-41

At the moment, I'm uncertain when I return to England, but I will let you know later.

Yours very sincerely

William Walton

After the first complete performance one of the most enthusiastic letters came from another composer, John Ireland (3 March 1936): 'It was the kind of performance any composer would envy, & Walton is very lucky to have such an interpreter of his work, which in your hands impresses me as the finest British work since Elgar.' Indeed, composers did not leave Harty in any doubt as to their appreciation of their good fortune in having him as their interpreter. The relationship of Granville Bantock and Harty seems to have been conducted on a consistent level of light-hearted fooling (a letter dated 12 March 1927 begins 'My dear old O'Harty' and ends 'ever yours McBan.'), but a performance of 'Omar Khayyám' in 1924 moved Bantock to ecstatic seriousness — ending however with a promise that 'our banter shall be resumed in the next letter — at our next meeting'. (10 February 1924)

But Harty's relations with composers did not always remain on such an even keel. With E. J. Moeran things went well at the start, but on 8 September 1937 Moeran had to explain to Harty how it had come about that his symphony (promised to Harty) was now to be conducted by someone else. He explains in great detail and at great length — for some nine pages in fact — then invites Harty to accept the dedication of it, and finally tries to interest him in his new violin concerto. We do not have Harty's reply, but the tone and content of it is quite evident from Moeran's next letter:

Norwich, 17 September 1937

My dear Harty,

Thank you for your letter. I think you must have misunderstood mine; I had no intention of bothering you with the score of my violin concerto. In fact, the ultimate production of it is quite in the air, so far as I am concerned, for it is not yet finished, & it may be a year or more before I am sufficiently satisfied with it to think of the question of a performance. If you still have my letter, please have another look at that part of it; but perhaps I expressed myself badly. But surely you must realize that I would not ask you to take up a piece of that nature, especially in view of this muddle over the Symphony.

82

'Dear Sir Hamilton': Letters 1915-41

It is a terrible disappointment to me that you do not feel inclined to accept the dedication...

— and so on for another page and a bit, with an afterthought winding its way up the margin as well. If Moeran doth protest too much, Joseph Holbrooke is forever furious, and an erratic typist to boot:

Author's Club, 19 February [1940?]

Dear Harty

I,ve waited so long to hear my No 3 "Ships" Symphony- that I now give it up as hopeless. All you boys- with a bl---- War on are still conducting foreign music as mush as ever- as you know. Well- would you be a good chap- and return the scores I sent you? They are not plentiful- and I value them. No doubt- you would never be allowed to conduct them anyway. The same applies to Wood.

Such an "EMPIRE"- as ours is a scandal in music- and fighting for a lifetime to alter this- is a bitter pill-as I,ve done my best to focus OUR WORKS- but the "school tie" boys hav have defeated me. Last War- just the same.

Dig those scores out- no good to you.

AND this bl--- Parliament of ours--listening to Hitlers yells for 1o years- & doing NOTHING. GOD.

warm regards from
Holbrooke.

Of course, a man in Harty's position was inundated with scores from hopeful composers, and he could not possibly perform them all. Of the foreign composers the one whose cause he championed with most enthusiasm was Sibelius, who in acknowledging his indebtedness managed a pun as well:

Helsingfors, 11 October 1934

Dear Sir Hamilton,

my hearty thanks for your very kind letter. I was immensely pleased about it. Let me express my profound gratitude to you for the interest and understanding you have always shown my music. During years I have followed your work and it was always with great satisfaction I knew my music to be in your masterful hands. Feeling happy about the opportunity to say to you this I beg you to accept my best regards.

Yours sincerely
Jean Sibelius

The revelatory experience of Harty's Berlioz performances brought him a hugh amount of mail from people in all walks of life. The music of Berlioz has always tended to produce strong reactions one way or the other, and reading these letters reveals how wide the gulf was in the 1920s and '30s between the Berlioz fanatics and those who simply could not understand him. One self-confessed 'fanatical admirer of Berlioz' was Sacheverell Sitwell. As a postscript to an enthusiastic letter dated 18 November 1930 he writes 'I am always wondering what the "Berlioz problem" is. To an amateur ear, like my own, there does not seem to be any problem at all, and nothing except unqualified success.' After the big Berlioz concert on 4 March 1936 Sitwell wrote again:

Towcester, 7 March 1936

My dear Harty
Your concert was superb and wonderful. I do not believe there is another musician alive, German, Italian, or Russian who could have done it.
How maddening the 'Times' has been: it is a somnambulist paper and fell asleep long before 1840, or whenever the Symphonie funèbre et trionphale was written.
Next year I do hope you will give 'La Impériale': and the 'Menace of the Franks', which Wootton says in his book has a magnificent march. Don't bother to answer this note, as it is only to tell you how much everyone in the audience enjoyed the concert. I cannot think the 'Tuba Mirum' ever sounded more terrifying.
Yours ever
Sacheverell Sitwell

The reference to *The Times* was prompted by H. C. Colles's review of the concert, one of the few that were less than enthusiastic. Harty wrote to Colles about it and Colles replied with a detailed self-defence (8 March), concluding: 'If I used my conviction to warn people off Berlioz it would be wrong, but I don't. I think you perfectly right to do his works and to use all your conviction to display them at their best to the public & I congratulate you on a very fine achievement.'

Another ardent Berliozian was Bernard van Dieren. Van Dieren was keen for Harty to give 'authentic' performances and wrote (12 February 1931): 'You had some correspondence with my very dear friend Heseltine — whose executor I am — concerning ophicleides.' Philip Heseltine ('Peter Warlock') indeed had written to Harty several years earlier, on 21 January 1927. In beautiful tiny hand-

'Dear Sir Hamilton': Letters 1915-41

writing on tiny sheets of notepaper he began 'I feel I must write and thank you for the wonderful experience of Thursday night's performance' and eventually got on to the subject of ophicleides:

At the end of the "Hosanna" the four ophicleides, *without* the trombones doubling them, must have sounded amazing. As they are nearly always doubled elsewhere, either in the octave or in unison, this passage must have been intended as a special effect.

A Grenadier Guards bandsman told me the other day that two members of the band learned the ophicleide some years ago and played it at, I think, the Military Tournament — or it may have been some historical pageant. If you ever feel inclined to try the instruments in performance, these men could probably manage the parts. I still have my ophicleide which is always at your disposal; and if more than one should be wanted, I know there are two at least at Potters', in West Street, Cambridge Circus. But one would probably be hard put to it to find an *"Ophicléide monstre avec pistons"* at this time of day!

With many thanks again, and all good wishes for future triumphs,

I remain

Ever yours sincerely

Philip Heseltine

Another Harty fan was George Bernard Shaw. After one of the 1930 'Hamilton Harty Symphony Concerts' at which Elgar's Symphony in E flat was the main item he wrote:

London, 25 January 1930

Dear Sir Hamilton Harty,

On expressing a desire a few days ago to hear last night's concert I was surprised by the news that you had sent me tickets for the whole series and had written me a personal letter therewith on the 19th October. I am assured that this came before me with my other letters; so I must plead guilty either of a lapse of consciousness or some careless shuffle of papers in which it got sidetracked. Anyhow, the apparent rudeness, and the crime of keeping two stalls empty on so many occasions, were unintended, though they lie none the lighter on my conscience.

The symphony went wonderfully: I heard everything in it with the last inch of effect. The great rampage in the rondo came off with indescribable completeness. And you know how very seldom that can be said of an orchestral performance, especially in London, where the players are so clever that they can read everything and consequently never know anything. I have always said that we should get no really satisfactory performances of such works as those of Elgar and Berlioz until they were played without notes, not read. You produced that effect last night: the band seemed to be really in possession of the music. How you knocked it into them, and got it out of them,

85

Heaven knows. I can only guess six months rehearsal. Anyhow it was so magnificent that I have written a line to Elgar about it.

My wife was enchanted, and reviled me for not having made her come to all the other concerts. She declares, by the way, that all the Manchester players have precisely similar noses, and she wants to know whether you select them by that feature, as she thought that their ears were the important organs.

As we met Lady Hamilton Harty at Madeira, and she seemed to like us, perhaps we shall have the pleasure of making your personal acquaintance some day when you are not too busy — if that ever happens.

Faithfully
G. Bernard Shaw

Shaw did write to Elgar the same day with a glowing account of the performance, and this has fortunately been published elsewhere.[4] A considerable amount of the surviving correspondence comes from the soloists with whom Harty performed: Busoni looks forward to reading the play by Synge given him by Harty (2.3.21); Rakhmaninov recommends Medtner as a pianist and composer (28.6.22); Frederic Lamond looks forward to the concert but is sick of playing the 'Emperor' — couldn't it be the Fourth instead? (17.7.22); Guilhermina Suggia insists that she does not use a string shopping bag(!); Formichi hopes that his letter of thanks will be published (5.3.26); Cassadó is enthusiastic about Harty's cello pieces (22.10.28); Maggie Teyte puts her *cachet* at 75 guineas but will bring it down to 60; Myra Hess insists that a 'somewhat demonstrative gesture' made in the afterglow of a great musical experience was quite unpremeditated (13.12.32); Kreisler finds Harty's Violin Concerto very fresh and charming; Szigeti sums up the feelings of all of them — 'It is a joy to think of music-making in the atmosphere that you create around you' (22.2.31). Koussevitsky, Ivor Novello, Stanford, Alexander Mackenzie, Nelson Eddy, Edward Dent and Robert Nicholls are just a few of the strange mixture of names represented in Harty's correspondence. Moira O'Neill and W. B. Yeats are glad for him to set their verse in his 'Five Irish Poems' of 1938, while Henry Wood solicits his support in arranging his own (i.e. Wood's) jubilee celebrations (3.9.37).

Three of his closest friends were Michele Esposito, John

4. Percy M. Young, *Elgar O.M.* (London, 1955), 377-8.

Harty and Myra Hess during a rehearsal break

McCormack and W. H. Squire, and their chatty, homely letters (beginning 'Dear Hay' [5] rather than 'Dear Sir Hamilton') are quite different in tone from those with whom his relationship was primarily a musical one. Esposito's daughter Vera wrote a touching letter after her father's death on 19 November 1929 and both McCormack and Squire sent him cheering letters just days before his own death. And then there are letters from numerous people whose names will be found in no reference book. There is one letter, undated and unsigned, which deserves quotation here since it so eloquently expresses the pleasure and enrichment that Harty brought to the lives of countless people. After a successful concert, who could ask for more?

Dear Sir

I want to thank you and your musicians, as you seem absolutely one, for the gorgeous programme of orchestral music we have heard this past season. I look forward to your concerts all the week as I work very hard, and they are more than a joy to remember. On Thursday evenings I get into my enchanted castle and bang the door on a sometimes very dreary world. Thank *you* with all my heart, for you are the life and soul of it all! It's a grand thing to be able to give so much happiness to so many people. Please *dont* ever let them shorten the programmes by 5 minutes!

I dont sign my name because you are a busy man & dont want to write notes and my name conveys nothing so why write it?

This winter your concerts were the bright spot in a hard heavy time. God bless you and yours and make you as happy as you make others.

5. In her contribution to a broadcast programme about Harty in 1951 Lady Harty (Agnes Nicholls) explained the origin of this nickname: 'Some people used to call him, as a joke, ''Hale and Harty'', and that very soon was reduced to ''Hayland''. But after I started calling him ''Hay'', everybody quickly followed suit; and ever after that, his intimate friends always called him ''Hay''.'

VII   ORCHESTRAL MUSIC

Raymond Warren

The first thing to be said of Harty's orchestral music is how very clearly it shows the advantages to a composer of being also a conductor; for the orchestration is brilliant and resourceful and he has an unerring instinct as to what will come off well in performance. Take a marvellous moment like the transformation in 'The Children of Lir', when Finola is turned from a swan back into human form. When one hears her theme in a new ethereal scoring in double octaves in the strings, supported by gently undulating brass chords and with little cascades of sound in the background tossed around by the woodwind to suggest the continuing presence of the sea below the cliff top, one can also picture Harty on the rostrum listening with an acute ear for every detail of the texture.

But there were disadvantages too. For one thing his busy life as a conductor can have left him all too little of the quiet time for renewal a composer needs: his output slowed considerably as his conducting responsibilities increased and it is rather sad that the composition of 'The Children of Lir', arguably his finest work, was perhaps only made possible by the serious illness which kept him away from the rostrum. On a deeper level too there is a fundamental difference of outlook between a conductor who must keep in the front of his mind a wide repertoire, every detail of which he must transmit to his immediate audience, and a composer who must work on a sustained single vision. Between two such different activities there was bound to be a tension and one must be sympathetic to it if one is to understand Harty's achievement, which was nevertheless to be the most important Irish composer of his generation. And if in this sphere he did not equal his greatness as a conductor, perhaps because of the way he chose to allocate the priorities of his time, the two activities together certainly add up to an impressive life's achievement.

Before embarking on a discussion of each work in the chronological order of its composition, we may see his output in clearer perspective by considering the three categories into which the principal works fall: the Irish works ('With the Wild Geese', Irish Variations, Irish Symphony and 'The Children of Lir'),[1] the 'classical' works (the two concertos, Comedy Overture and 'Fantasy Scenes') and thirdly the transcriptions of music by Handel and Field.

The first category of Irish music includes, I suspect, those works which were closest to the composer's heart. Although almost all he wrote has a certain Irish flavour it was in these overtly Irish pieces that he came nearest to expressing his deep love of his native country, no doubt made the more poignant by his having to work elsewhere. For a country with no full-time professional orchestra was hardly the place for an aspiring young conductor and no doubt this lack was one of the factors militating against the establishment earlier in the century of an Irish national school of composition, a surprising loss to music in view of the wealth of characteristic folksong and the strength of national feeling in Ireland, which produced such fruits in poetry and drama. But the fact was that, like Stanford before him, Harty was bound to leave Ireland to pursue a musical career to his own standards. Like Stanford, too, Harty's musical nationalism was a matter of interpreting an Irish experience within the terms of the Anglo-European musical language as he then understood it — the approach of Smetana and Rimsky-Korsakov rather than of Bartók or Vaughan Williams. In musical terms this was a matter of nationalism in melody rather than in harmony, which was in the broad European Romantic tradition and generally speaking diatonic or chromatic even when the melody was modal.

Of the two tone poems, both inspired by splendid subjects from Irish legend, the earlier one, 'With the Wild Geese', had a poignancy new to Harty's own music and also to Irish music in general; 'The Children of Lir' was virtually Harty's swan song and also, having been written as late as 1938, a swan song of the grand Romantic tone poem. Cast in a single movement over thirty minutes long, it is his most ambitious structure. The Irish Symphony — a

1. To this group might be added the Fantasy for flute and piano 'In Ireland' (1918), which he arranged for flute, harp and orchestra in 1935 (see p. 131), and the arrangement of 'The Londonderry Air'.

rather less weighty piece despite its title — shows a quite different kind of nationalism, being based largely on folk melodies. It is perhaps worth noting that the two tone poems are cast in almost palindromic forms of the type ABCBA, unlike Harty's other orchestral music almost all of which is in traditional sonata or ternary forms.

The group I have designated his 'classical' works are perhaps less what Parry would have called 'characteristic' than the first group but they are all highly effective concert pieces in the mainstream Romantic tradition. Their harmonic language is basically within the Dvořák-Rimsky-Korsakov orbit, and like much music of the late 19th century they tend to be organized in symmetrical two- or four-bar phrase structures. Their directness of appeal is partly due to their eschewing the German manner of contrapuntal motivic development and relying mostly on simpler melody and accompaniment textures: Harty had a great facility for continuous melodic invention supported by accompaniments delightfully varied to keep up the interest. One may indeed feel that his gift as a songwriter lay in the very heart of his orchestral composition, and this is perhaps relevant to his tendency towards a lyrical nostalgia which would sound English, almost Elgarian, if it were not for the Irish flavour.

The Comedy Overture in particular deserves to be played more: it has those qualities of wit, brilliance and sentiment which were characteristic of Harty as a person. The two concertos are fine examples of brilliant solo writing with skilful orchestral accompaniment and balance. The 'Fantasy Scenes' and the unpublished 'Singer of Shiraz' music show yet another side of his work, an accomplished oriental style in the tradition of Rimsky-Korsakov's 'Scheherezade'.[2] Harty's further versatility can be found in the convincing Scottish idioms of the incidental music to 'Proud Maisie'.

The fashion nowadays dictates either a high degree of authenticity in the performance of early music, or else a more radical re-fashioning of the original. Harty's transcriptions, which enjoyed great

---

2. On a more local level, Harty's oriental style reflects the cult of the exotic which was a feature of British music and literature in the early years of the century — one thinks of Holst and Bantock and (among writers) James Elroy Flecker.

popularity in their day, seem now to fall between the two stools. They are in fact comparatively straightforward arrangements of the originals for the modern symphony orchestra. The harmonies of the Handel works are enriched by fuller scoring (in particular Harty's warm use of his four horns gives a certain Romantic glow to the music) and sevenths may be added to dominant chords, but the essentials of the music, its melody and continuo harmony are rarely altered more than this. One cannot help feeling that Harty and his contemporaries would have been astonished at a change of fashion which rejects these restrained orchestrations, and Mozart's too for that matter, and yet can enjoy 'Pulchinella'! These comments are less applicable to the 'John Field Suite' which is for chamber orchestra and, written at the very end of his life, reflects something of the changing fashion.

But we must thank Harty for the fact that the 'Water Music' in particular has assumed its rightful place in our national musical heritage. This is surely another example of how his knowledge, from the rostrum, of what his orchestra would like to play and his audience to hear, gave a timely stimulus to his compositional skills.

* * *

The overture 'The Exile' exists in a manuscript score bearing no date, but the designation op.2 must mean 1900-1. There are rather a lot of small errors such as missed accidentals, suggesting in the absence of evidence to the contrary that the work was never performed. The presence of a number of pencilled revisions suggests that he may have re-written it after perhaps showing it to Esposito. A rather morbid poem of the same title by Thomas Campbell is copied out in Harty's hand on the second page, describing a dying exile's wish to bless his native land. Evidently the young Harty saw the expressive rather than the nationalistic possibilities of the subject for after a sombre introduction the Allegro has a distinctly Mendelssohnian flavour (ex.1). Naturally in reading through the score with historical hindsight one is looking out for early signs of his Irish melodic gifts, and one will not be disappointed by the second subject, written in the score for oboe but surely intended for the clarinet (ex.2). The change to a slower tempo at this point exemplifies an expressive device which was to become a mannerism of many of his sonata form movements. The overture closes dramatically with a reversion to slower notes reminiscent of the introduction.

Ex.1

Ex.2

An Irish Symphony, perhaps Harty's most direct and tuneful work, was evidently the one to give him the most trouble to compose, for it is known to have existed in three distinct versions. The first of them won the *Feis Ceoil* prize in Dublin in 1904 and although the score is now lost a *Musical Times* review in March 1916[3] states that like the later versions it contained the tunes 'The Croppy Boy', 'The Blackberry Blossom', 'The Boyne Water', 'Drahereen-o-Machree' ('Jimín Mo Mhíle Stór') and 'The Girl I left behind Me'. In composing it Harty may have had in mind the Irish symphonies of Sullivan and Stanford, and perhaps especially the one by his teacher Esposito, which was performed in Dublin in December 1902, after having itself won the *Feis Ceoil* prize earlier that year.

Harty gave his score a thoroughgoing revision for a performance he conducted himself in Leeds in 1916, and presumably that is the version of the manuscript score dated 1915 now in the Queen's University library. He revised it further for a Hallé performance in 1924, and only now were the programme notes and titles to the movements added. This was the version published by Boosey in 1927. Although

3. *The Musical Times*, lvii (1916), 166.

there were again many alterations, these were mostly matters of comparative detail which did not change the basic conception of the previous version.

The basing of a symphony on folksongs certainly saves the composer the problem of having to invent memorable themes: as ex.3 shows, this symphony positively abounds in them! However it can

Ex.3

These tunes are I(a) Avenging and Bright
          I(b) The Croppy Boy
          II(a) Reel: The Blackberry Blossom
          II(b) The Girl I left behind Me
          III   Jimín Mo Mhíle Stór
          IV   Boyne Water

create more problems than it saves, bearing in mind the adage that the only thing to do with a good tune is to repeat it. Harty got round the problem with his usual technical fluency, sometimes by extending the tune himself and then developing his extension (melodically of course — as with most of his music the prevailing texture is melody and accompaniment), or he may work a figure from the folksong itself, though not necessarily from its opening. He makes use of both these devices in the first movement ('On the Shores of Lough Neagh') to extend the theme I(a) into a symphonic first subject, getting away from the theme with a development of his own continuation of it and coming back with a codetta based on the motif (x) to round off the section and prepare for his second subject I(b).

The second movement, 'The Fair Day', is the scherzo of the symphony and it shows Harty's lightness of touch and his humour at its very best. The pace does not relax, from the fiddler's tuning-up in the introduction to the delicious soft xylophone glissandi at·the end, a touch of self-deprecating humour very characteristic of an Ulsterman! Another nice touch is the use of 'The Girl I left behind Me', a tune whose Irish origins have been open to some doubt. Indeed there was a lively controversy on the subject in the pages of *The Musical Times* in 1913 when the irrepressible Dr. Grattan Flood, arguing for the Irishness of the tune, seemed to get the worst of the argument.[4] So Harty's retention of the tune in the 1915 version, where it is heard to grow so naturally out of the indisputably Irish reel 'The Blackberry Blossom', gives Grattan Flood some unscholarly but very convincing support!

The slow movement, 'In the Antrim Hills', described by Harty as 'a wistful lament' is based entirely on the beautiful 'Jimín Mo Mhíle Stór', which is extended and ornamented in the manner of an improvisation.

The finale is the most problematical movement of the symphony. Its title 'The 12th of July' refers of course to the Protestant festival celebrating the Battle of the Boyne, hence the appropriateness of the main theme 'The Boyne Water', which is played to this day by the flute bands in the processions of the Orangemen. That the festive

---

4. *The Musical Times*, liv (1913), 309, 516, 598.

atmosphere is splendidly evoked goes without saying. Harty did however give himself a difficult task in attempting a symphonic finale for a work whose previous movements have been so individually colourful and contrasted and it is evident from the more extensive nature of the revisions to this movement that he found it the most difficult part of the symphony to get right. We might think of the problem as that of the movement's having sufficient weight to be the culmination of the symphony but also a sufficient identity with the other movements to integrate the whole work.

He achieved the weight by writing another sonata-type movement with original secondary material and by a big coda: and he achieved the integration, perhaps less successfully, by introducing into the movement music from the scherzo and the slow movement. Indeed in the 1924 version the symphony actually finishes with a third and majestic reappearance of theme III, where in the 1915 version it finished with a *vivace* coda growing out of II(a). One feels that in the 1924 version he puts too much weight on that tender slow melody and that the coda is the one place where the 1915 version is preferable. For the rest of the movement however, and indeed the other movements too, a comparison of the two versions gives a fascinating glimpse of a fine craftsman at work, pointing the melodies with more piquant ornamentation or phrasing, making small cuts to tighten the structure, clarifying the textures with more effective scorings or accompaniment figurations and, perhaps most frequently of all, simply enriching the scoring so that the piece would communicate more easily to a big audience in a big hall: one might almost think of the conductor in him taking over now.

The manuscript score of the Comedy Overture is marked 'August 1906 rewritten Dec. 1908' (i.e. after its first performance in 1907), and this is the score used by Universal Edition for their engraving thirty years later. It had however been copyrighted by Schott in 1909. Harty labelled it op.15 on the manuscript but he had dropped this system of classification before the publication. The dedication is to Michele Esposito, who certainly had nothing more to teach his pupil now, for the work is technically most assured. Harty may have taken on more ambitious projects than this but he never did anything better: and if the subsequent revisions that he made to the

Irish Symphony show how uncertain he was of his path in 1904, in the Comedy Overture one senses that he has found his style. The Irish lilt and the pace of the opening theme (ex.4) scarcely let up for the whole work, though there is a more lyrical second subject which illustrates Harty's essentially diatonic harmony (ex.5). The continuation of this theme with an almost Elgarian sequential pattern is perhaps the least characteristic music in the overture (ex.6). A com-

parison of this with ex.18 will show how he was using similar melodic material with more character in his later works. However the continual orchestral invention never allows the interest to flag, for although there is a good deal of melodic repetition when the opening phrases of the theme are developed, the orchestral settings are never exactly repeated. Of many possible examples of orchestral virtuosity one might single out the 'false recapitulation', when the orchestral build-up leads to a comic statement of ex.4 in the wrong key on a piccolo high above a deep drone on two bassoons. Calling the miscreant instruments to order the timpani batter out the opening six notes of the theme in the right key, twice for good measure. Only then can the orchestra prepare itself for the proper recapitulation on solo clarinet — a really Haydnesque piece of humour, despite the fact that it is said that he had little interest in Haydn![5]

The Violin Concerto in D minor was written in 1908-9 for a first performance by Szigeti in the Queen's Hall, and a violin-and-piano version was published by Schott in 1909. The full score was published by C.E. Music Publishers in 1920. That this very skilful work was composed with Szigeti and the international musical world in mind is further borne out by the fact that of all his major works this one is the least Irish in character. One thinks of it as being of the school of Dvořák, whose Cello Concerto was written a decade earlier. Perhaps it was a desire to redress the balance which led Harty to write his Irish Variations for the same medium only a few years later.

A short introductory passage is based on a semiquaver figure which soon finds its place in the opening theme of the vigorous first movement (ex.7); and where in other works we might have looked out for an Irish flavour to the second subject we have here something distinctly Brahmsian (ex.8), an impression strengthened by the passages in parallel thirds and sixths which follow. The main theme of the lyrical slow movement has a touch of distinction because of the falling leading notes (ex.9). After some opening solo violin rhetoric in the true Wieniawsky tradition the vivacious last movement theme scampers along to a repeated-note accompaniment on the horns, the excitement of which is equalled by a new and inventive accompaniment for the theme each time it reappears (ex.10).

The success of this work, added to that of the 'Ode to a Nightingale' and the Comedy Overture undoubtedly put Harty in English

5. John F. Russell, 'Hamilton Harty', *Music & Letters*, xxii (1941), 220.

eyes among the most promising young composers of the day. If we think the piece rather conservative for such a distinction we must remember that England in the wake of the Romantic movement was

a conservative place, and that the new winds blowing on the continent — the works of Debussy and the younger composers Stravinsky, Bartók and Schoenberg — were not to make an impact on English concert life for some time yet. It seems however that the concerto's success did not entirely satisfy the young composer himself, who moved in an unexpected direction for his next big work; unexpected that is for those unaware of the unpublished 'The Exile' and Irish Symphony, to whose world he now returned, but having acquired a much greater technical assurance. The inspiration seems to have been poetry again, this time a volume of verse by the Hon Emily Lawless, published in 1902.

Ex.11

'With the Wild Geese', a poem for orchestra, was first performed at the Cardiff Festival of 1910 and published by Novello in 1912. Two poems by Emily Lawless are printed at the head of the score, the first describing the night before the battle of Fontenoy (1745) in the wars of the Austrian succession and in which some Irish regiments were helping their old French allies. In the second poem, subtitled 'After the Battle; Early Dawn, Clare Coast', the ghosts of the slain soldiers are seen returning over the sea to their homeland. The poem takes the form of a conversation between the ghost soldiers and a questioning Irish observer, a dialogue structure which perhaps suggested the antiphonal nature of some of the musical development.

As will be apparent from ex.11, all the main themes have an affinity to Irish folksongs (though they are in fact original) and all bear a certain family likeness. Harty in his own programme note suggests that the slow introduction A depicts the exiles' farewell to Ireland and B the life of the Irish Brigade abroad. Theme C represents the exiles' dreams of home. The conflict between the battle fanfares and those Irish themes have a clear programmatic meaning, as have the later transformations of the themes to suggest nocturnal or ghostly events. Indeed the skill of Harty's orchestral techniques in accomplishing these transformations is a remarkable feature of the work. Another is the melodic invention which extends the melodies, often with two- or four-bar sequential patterns, but keeping to their general style, so that they can lead smoothly one into another. The loose thematic integration, continuous melody, strong emotional undercurrents in the harmonies and the quite unashamed playing for melodramatic effect from time to time, all give the music a certain affinity to Puccini.

Ex.12

The Variations on a Dublin Air for violin and orchestra are sometimes known as the 'Irish Variations' though in the unpublished manuscript of 1912 Harty seems to have erased the second title. He turned now to something very different from the previous work but equally Irish. The theme is a traditional melody 'The Valley lay smiling before Me', originally called 'The Young Girl Milking her Cow', and Harty probably got it from Moore. Ex.12 gives the first few bars of the melody and of the first two variations to show with what skill he could invent characteristic Irish melody within the disciplines of the given outline. There are seven variations in all, of which the last begins with a restatement of the opening slow introduction. The invention seems to flag somewhat in the middle, for example in the rather academic fugato of the fifth variation, and it is known that Harty had intended revising the work, though he never found time to do so. This is a pity because it has a characteristic warm lyricism which should earn it a place in the repertoire of short works for the medium.

The 'Proud Maisie' incidental music was written for a play based on Sir Walter Scott's 'The Heart of Midlothian':[6] the unpublished manuscript score is dated 1912. There are eight movements in all of which the largest, the overture, is one of Harty's most spirited pieces, with some fine sweeping melodies in 4/4 time and of Scottish flavour set against a lively 12/8 dance with the suggestion of bag-pipes in the scoring. One of the movements is a song 'The White Cockade' and another a funeral march, both thematically related to the overture. The final music is mostly soft chords as a background to the final speech of the play.

'The Singer of Shiraz' incidental music consists of twelve move-ments for a play by James B. Fagan, the unpublished manuscript dating from 1915 (see p. 75). Harty has matched the atmosphere of this oriental romance with suitably colourful and exotic music scored for small orchestra. Five of the movements are songs.

'Fantasy Scenes from an Eastern Romance' is a suite for small orchestra, a pleasant piece of light music composed or assembled in 1919 for a first performance and publication (by C.E.) in 1920. Harty has suggested on the score a programmatic basis for the music, a rather slight oriental love story with something of the 'Arabian Nights' atmosphere, and so he makes further use of the oriental style of 'The Singer of Shiraz'. Indeed the third movement is simply a re-scoring for solo horn of the third movement of the earlier work, there a violin solo. There are four movements: 'The Laughing Juggler' has

6. The title 'Proud Maisie' comes from the song that Madge Wildfire sings on her deathbed (chap. 39).

the expected vivacious writing; 'A Dancer's Reverie' is an attractive movement with delicate staccato writing contrasted with melodic arabesques in the middle section; then comes 'Lonely in Moonlight' and finally the colourful 'In the Slave Market'.

The 'Suite for Orchestra (from the Water Music)' was first performed in 1920 and published by Murdoch in 1922. Harty offered it to Murdoch (at the suggestion of Arnold Bax) only after it had been rejected by several other publishers on the grounds that it would not sell. This first of Harty's Handel arrangements has remained the most popular of them probably because of the consistently high quality of the originals, plus the fact that Harty, who knew his audience, showed great perception in selecting and ordering the movements so as to make an attractive concert item.

Handel's original 'Water Music' included two orchestral suites: in F (and D minor), scored for horns, oboes, bassoon and strings, and in D major, the key for the trumpets he added. Harty took his first five movements from the first suite and the final one from the second. He scored for a full modern woodwind section in place of Handel's oboes and bassoon and his standard four horns in place of Handel's two. He keeps close to Handel's general orchestral layout and use of contrasted orchestrations even though his range of available colours is so much greater: indeed the fidelity to Handel and the general restraint are noteworthy. He even makes a virtue of keeping to Handel's general trumpet scorings, for his first four movements in F are followed by an Andante in D minor which serves as an introduction to his final Allegro in D major. Thus tonally the music curves round from F to the brighter key of D and by saving his trumpets for the only movement in which Handel used them he reinforces his unusual tonal shape and gives a climactic finish to his suite.

The skill of selection to which I referred is well illustrated by his decision to omit the original opening movement — a fine but rather formal French overture — and to begin with Handel's third[7] movement whose slow harmonies, arising from its repeated chord figure, give the music a wonderfully spacious opening. The Air which

---

7. The ordering of Handel's movements is here taken from Chrysander's complete edition.

follows was originally the sixth movement, to which for a middle section Harty effectively couples the F minor trio section of Handel's seventh movement. The striking horn solos in the recapitulation, growing out of long held notes, are a remarkable feature of the original too, though when Harty extends Handel's coda for a few bars by repeating the first phrase of the Air on his four muted horns he makes a gorgeous but rather un-Handelian sound! Two short quick movements, Bourrée and Hornpipe, played in succession as in Handel, make an effective Scherzo for Harty's suite before the D minor Andante leads into the final Allegro deciso. This splendid addition to the concert repertoire was welcomed by everyone, not excepting the writers of programme notes who could recount the picturesque but apocryphal story of Handel's first performance.

The Concerto in B minor for Pianoforte and Orchestra, dedicated to Michele Esposito, was first performed in Leeds in 1922 and published by C.E. Music Publishers (the Dublin firm run by Sir Stanley Cochrane and Esposito) in 1923.[8] It reverts, particularly in the first two movements, to the general idiom of the Violin Concerto, though it has a greater breadth and a heavier Romanticism than the earlier concerto: indeed there is a combination of eloquent, sweeping melody and intense, often chromatic harmonies, giving it an affinity with the concertos of Rakhmaninov. Like them, too, it has a brilliant and rewarding piano part, reminding us that Harty's eminence as a pianist was yet another facet of this remarkable musician.

Ex.13

Something of the *appassionato* quality of the first movement can be sensed from the opening theme with its strong rising and falling sixths (ex.13). The slow movement has for its main theme a sustained and tranquil cantilena which with its lovely diatonic sequence is surely one of his most beautiful creations (ex.14). The quiet intro-

8. The concerto was also performed on two pianos at a reception in Dublin in 1925 on the occasion of Harty's being awarded an Honorary MusD.

duction to the movement reappears from time to time as a punctuation to the main melody, rather like the ritornello of a song. After a quicker middle section the final appearance of the main melody has beautifully embellished figurations in the accompaniment, and then the music of the introduction forms a peaceful coda.

Ex.14

Ex.15

The last movement occupies a very different world indeed. The vigorous main theme is built as surely on fifths as the first movement was on sixths (ex.15), but this time there is a very pronounced Irish quality, a close similarity in fact to the second variation of the

'Dublin Air' (ex.12). Harty, in his own programme note written for a performance at a Hallé concert in 1923, even suggested that the movement might be taken to describe a scene in 'an Irish tavern with drinking, dancing and general gaiety'. If so the company is certainly varied, for after a rather Brahmsian second subject in 6/4 time the music quietens dramatically for a veiled statement on muted horns of a phrase from the old Irish partisan song 'The Wearing of the Green', and indeed after due recapitulation of the other material a further phrase of the same tune is played *fortissimo* on the brass, with Tchaikovsky-like impassioned harmonies. The indulging in such unsophisticated humour makes the movement exceptional in Harty's output: needless to say the scoring makes it all very exciting to listen to.

The 'Suite from the Music for the Royal Fireworks', composed in 1923 and published by Murdoch in the following year, was clearly intended as a follow-up to the successful 'Water Music'. Handel's original scoring was most spectacular: 28 oboes, 9 horns, 9 trumpets, 12 bassoons, and strings, though this involved much doubling and a performance with reduced numbers would have been perfectly feasible. Harty, evidently thinking out the problem afresh for such a transcription, decided to keep to Handel's basic colours by dispensing with his flutes and clarinets, but to keep to the usual standard numbers of the other wind. Although he keeps often to the general outlines of Handel's scorings, there is less exact doubling of wind with wind or wind with strings, and he more frequently indulges in small changes of colour. He chose four movements from Handel's original suite, as follows:

Overture: the French overture from the original but omitting Handel's final *Lentement*. Having thus ended with a quick movement instead of a slow one he now reversed the order of Handel's next two movements.

Alla Siciliana: called by Handel 'La Paix'.

Bourrée: as in Handel, but repeating the final phrase to make a small coda.

Orchestral Music

Menuetto: Harty took Handel's sixth movement, a majestic minuet in D major, and used Handel's fifth movement, another minuet in D minor, as its trio.

His next Handelian arrangement, the 'Polonaise, Arietta and Passacaglia' was first performed in America in 1932 and published by Boosey in the same year. It consists of orchestral transcriptions of three rather oddly matched movements: a Polonaise in G from the Concerto Grosso for strings in E minor, op.6 no.3, scored for full orchestra without trumpets; an Arietta, a rather unusual scoring for flute, bassoons, horns and strings of the aria 'Si che lieta goderò' from the opera 'Rodrigo'; and finally a scoring for full orchestra with three trumpets of the Passacaille, the last section of the 'Rodrigo' overture. In fact, he had already arranged these three movements (along with other Handel pieces) for violin and piano many years earlier, and it is interesting to observe how his Handel arrangements 'progressed' from chamber music to orchestral proportions as his career as a conductor took over from that of accompanist.

The 'Concerto for Orchestra with Organ (G. F. Handel)' was published by Universal in 1934 and recorded by Columbia that November. It is for the most part a scoring of the second of three Handel orchestral concertos based on the same material (Concerto 'B' in *Händel-Gesellschaft* edition ed. F. Chrysander, xlvii), one of them being incorporated into the original 'Fireworks Music'. Quite unaccountably, unless he had received a special request for an organ work, Harty wrote a prominent organ part, though not really in the style or within the concept of an organ concerto.

The first movement is based on the opening Largo of the Handel concerto with the string parts omitted and played instead on the organ, giving the effect of antiphonal treatment between wind instruments and the organ. The second movement is a straightforward transcription of the final Allegro of the original Handel with no organ at all. At the final cadence of this Harty re-introduces six bars of the first movement, (which Handel does not do, though there is a different *Lentement* at the corresponding place in the 'Fireworks' version) leading without a break into his last movement (the second movement of the second Handel concerto), in which the organ now appears as a sort of continuo instrument and to add weight too. This piece is thus a curious hybrid in conception.

The 'Introduction and Rigaudon (G. F. Handel)' was published by Universal in 1935 and recorded together with the 'Polonaise, Arietta and Passacaglia' that December, so forming a five-movement suite. This further occasional piece is a transcription of two movements unrelated in theme, origin or scoring. The Introduction is an arrangement for solo string quartet and string orchestra of the second movement, in D minor, of Handel's Concerto Grosso for strings op.6 no.10. The antiphonal manner (though not in all details) of the original is preserved. 'Rigaudon' is Harty's title for the final dance movement of the overture to Handel's opera 'Ariodante', scored up for classical-sized symphony orchestra without clarinets.[9] This movement is in G minor.

Harty composed 'The Children of Lir, a Poem for Orchestra' in 1938 while he was convalescing from illness, and dedicated it to 'O.E.B.' (see p.64). He conducted its first performance at a BBC concert in March 1939, and it was published by Universal later that

Ex.16

Lento e con dignità

year. The work is based on one of the traditional 'Three Tragic Stories of Erin' and concerns King Lir's four children, whose jealous stepmother caused them to be turned into swans, to wander over Irish seas for a thousand years, only to return to their human shapes on hearing a Christian bell. One morning after many years of such wandering, they heard the bell of a church on a cliff top of County Antrim. Immediately they became human again, 'noble and beautiful still, but incredibly old'. The coast people took them to the church and baptised them before they died, burying them together

9. This is another piece that Harty had arranged for violin and piano, back in 1910.

in the churchyard overlooking the sea.

The music begins with a solemn chorale-like theme developed into a substantial and impressive introduction (ex.16). In his own programme note for the first performance, Harty interprets this as the thoughts of one who stands on the cliffs recalling the story (see p.59). One may perhaps feel that the church is part of the scene too, and that this introduction has something of the same relationship to the whole as the Friar Lawrence music in Tchaikovsky's 'Romeo and

Ex.17

Juliet'. A great many of Harty's instrumental movements have some sort of introduction, but none is so impressive as this, nor so powerful as in its reappearance at the end of the work.

The main theme of the ensuing Allegro describes 'the free open sea', and it is one of a group of themes of which another is also quoted to show something of the range of the section (ex.17). The sea with its varying moods, distant horizons and constant movement, is a magnificent subject for music, and here we may feel that Harty's orchestral virtuosity finds its finest fulfilment. Although he knew 'La Mer', having conducted it as far back as 1921, Harty's depiction of the sea is very different from Debussy's. In musical terms it is more song-like and tonal: expressing this in pictorial language we might perhaps think of it as viewed not from the depths of the sea itself but from the coast, and an Irish coast at that. Even the augmented triads of ex.17(b) are given a secure base by their regular sequence and phrase structure. After a while the pace of the music slackens for a lyrical second subject, a reflection on the 'passionate and sorrowful feelings of the swan-children', given melodic distinction by the three-bar phrase at the opening (ex.18). The melody shows how Harty achieves an Irish quality without being as self-conscious about it as he had to be, by the nature of the subject, in his earlier tone

Ex.18

poem. It also gives him several motifs by developing which he extends the section to the necessary length for its place in the structure.

We can think of the music so far as constituting an exposition, with the two main key centres in A and C. In the ensuring development we first hear some of the motifs of ex.18 alongside the sea music of ex.17 in a playful scherzando — 'for they were not always sorrowful, nor was the sea always rough and tempetuous'. Then the music quietens for a striking new idea, the entry of a soprano solo singing above an evocative orchestral harmony (ex.19). This represents Finola, the eldest of the swan-children, singing her 'plaintive song of weariness and of longing for the day of release'. The

pentatonic similarity of this to ex.18, and the use of the same ornamental figure as that of ex.17(b), give the feeling that this song
grows naturally out of the preceding music.

When the sea returns there is greater urgency and intensity: we
may perhaps think of this as a recapitulation since although the
themes of the ex.17 return in reverse order, the home key of A minor
is re-established with the big *forte* reappearance of ex.17(a). The
music grows to a fine climax into which Finola's song is heard again,
rising to a loud cry as the bell sounds and there takes place the
magical transformation described at the beginning of this chapter.
The return of the introductory music brings the work to a majestic
end.

Ex.19

Although so many years separate this work from Harty's previous
original work, it is evident that the suggestion of a move towards a
richer and darker Romanticism, noted in the Piano Concerto, now
comes to fruition. This is the biggest thing he wrote, and it needed
all his symphonic facility to sustain interest and formal purpose over
such a big canvas. There is of course his usual invention in the scoring, some splendid building up to climaxes and the seemingly endless facility by which no thematic recapitulation is ever an exact
repeat of another. He varies the overall shapes of the individual
sections too with great skill. The lyrical ones, using the themes of
ex.18 and 19 are self-contained, coming to a cadence in their own
home keys, but the other sections involving the 'sea' themes are
open-ended and always moving forwards to something new.

A page from Harty's copy of Field's Nocturne in B flat (Queen's University Library) with his pencilled annotations concerning the instrumentation

*The opening bars of the autograph score of the same Nocturne
('A John Field Suite')*

If one thinks of this as Harty's finest work, one is of course thinking of these technical matters and that here he stretched his powers
of symphonic development to their highest point. But even more one
is thinking of his achievement in having enshrined a national legend
in music. The programmatic elements, the intrusion of the solo
soprano, the sounding of the bell and the final transformation are
not only pictorially vivid, but they are as natural a part of the purely
musical argument as, say, the trumpet calls in 'Leonora' no.3. The

legend has flowered into symphony.

'A John Field Suite' was first performed and published (by Universal) in 1939.[10] This last of Harty's arrangements is rather different from the others. This time the music from which he started was for solo piano (piano quintet in the case of the last movement), unlike the Handel works which were all originally orchestral: he thus necessarily had a freer hand in re-thinking the music in orchestral terms. Another important difference is that Field, composing in the early days of the 19th century, was already at the beginning of the Romantic era to which as we have seen Harty in spirit really belonged. The two men have much in common despite the century between them; in their harmonic language, for example, and in their basic melody-plus-accompaniment texture. Field was an Irishman, too, and although this fact does not emerge in his piano music, it is noteworthy that when Harty transcribed the melodies in a perfectly straightforward way for orchestral instruments, he seems to show that they had an Irish flavour after all: one is thinking here of the theme of the Polka heard as a fiddle tune or the melodic ornamentation of the Nocturne given greater lyrical sostenuto in the woodwind. And finally in this list of differences, it is to be noticed that Harty was writing for a 'modern' chamber orchestra of single woodwind, horn, trumpet, percussion, harp and strings. He thus had the full range of orchestral colour for solo melodic work, but none of the rich Romantic choirs of wind available to him.

This transcription needs better playing than the others if it is to come over well in the concert hall, both because of the more exposed wind parts and also the necessarily small number of strings. The total effect of lightness, bright lines and clear textures gives the work an altogether different sound from the other arrangements. And although Harty limits himself almost entirely to orchestral techniques which might have been employed in Field's day, he nevertheless had in comparison with the Handel works a more creative role to play, and one in which he could immerse himself more naturally — a situation rather closer to that of 'Pulchinella' The titles and deriva-

10. As we have seen (see p.54), since about 1936 Harty had been planning to make some arrangements of music by Chopin. These never materialized, but it may well be that the interest in Field grew out of his study of Chopin — a natural enough transition, and a fitting tribute to a fellow-Irishman.

tions of the music are as follows: [11]

> Polka: the Rondo of the Sonata in E flat, op.1 no.1.
> Nocturne: the Nocturne no.5 in B flat.
> Slow Waltz 'Remembrance': Waltz in E 'Remembrance'.
> Rondo 'Midi': Rondo in E major for piano quintet, known as 'Le midi'.

There is clearly no question of comparing the achievement of this slight work with that of 'The Children of Lir'. But the two products of his last composing year make an interesting pair: the one a culmination and summary of his life's work, the other suggesting in its whimsical way that but for his untimely illness Harty might well have moved forwards as a composer in a fresh direction.

---

11. For full details of the sources of the movements see Cecil Hopkinson, *A Biblio-graphical Thematic Catalogue of the Works of John Field* (London, 1961).

VIII VOCAL MUSIC

Philip Cranmer

Before he became famous as a conductor Harty was already well known as an accompanist. And by no means the least of his qualities as a conductor was his gift for sympathetic accompaniment; a number of singers have told me that in his time he had no equal as an orchestral accompanist. It might therefore be presumed that his songs would be written from a pianist's point of view, with integral and important accompaniments. To a great extent this is true, though he hardly ever came near to Schumann's attitude. There is an occasional long introduction, but few codas that could be described as more than stitching the hem of the song. At the same time the accompaniments are never negligible and they are frequently of crucial importance. In the strophic songs they fulfil the duty, and often fulfil it with poetic insight, of creating variety between one verse and another, and of colouring outstanding words or phrases. The textures are in the 19th-century tradition of Romantic arpeggios and chord figures. There is hardly any of the percussive use of the instrument to which the 20th century has become accustomed — one might say inured.

As far as the vocal line is concerned Harty nearly always writes graceful and grateful melodies. Sometimes his long phrases recall Brahms, not so much in their outline as in the stringent demands which they make on the breath. There is an occasional arioso or even recitative-like contour, especially when a contemplative mood is needed, as in 'A Mayo Love Song' or the arrangement of 'My Lagan Love'. Not surprisingly the Irish songs have a modal or pentatonic flavour. Harty is always sensitive to the meaning of words, but oddly enough not always sufficiently careful or aware of their natural stresses. As can be seen from ex.20, he often prefers to retain a melodic line intact rather than modify it to assist the accentuation. 'An Irish Love Song' exhibits the same tendency, though here he does make a modification in the second verse (ex.21). The unpub-

116

lished full score of the 'Ode to a Nightingale' contains several pencilled alterations in Harty's own hand where he had second thoughts
about the accentuation of the text.

By far the largest number of Harty's songs were set to Irish poems.
Moira O'Neill heads the list with eleven, and Padraic Colum has
four. Yeats is represented only by 'The Fiddler of Dooney'. Of the
other poets who appear, Keats ('The Devon Maid') and Whitman
('By the bivouac's fitful flame') are the only really famous names,
and these two are represented in the longer vocal works, 'Ode to a
Nightingale' and 'The Mystic Trumpeter'. There is also a ballad for
chorus and orchestra to words by Whitman, 'Come up from the

fields father'. It survives only in manuscript with piano accompaniment, dated 1912. Among his early songs Harty set five poems from
the 16th and 17th centuries.[1] Here the music contains passages
which could easily have been written by Parry (thirty years senior to
Harty) or Quilter (just two years older than Harty). The songs are
none the worse for that; indeed Parry and Quilter are sometimes
seriously underrated. At the same time, in these settings Harty seems
to sacrifice some of his personality and to take refuge in an anonymous style. Further, he sometimes affects a turn of phrase of the sort
that Edward German and others popularized when an 'Elizabethan'
mood was required. The five songs are agreeable enough, but they
are not the real Harty.

The earliest published song is the 'Song of Glen Dun' (1902), to
words by Moira O'Neill. At first sight it is an ordinary song, but it
has some rhythmic interest, including a change of time-signature at
the refrain which softens the four-square metre of the verse. It has
also an appealing sigh at the end: 'Mother Mary, keep my love an'
send me my desire'.

Of the 1903 songs 'The Devon Maid' catches some of the arch
humour of Keats's poem, and 'Rose Madness' shows the first sign of
Harty's skilful touch in accompaniment. The outer sections are very
effective, but there is some pretentiousness in the chord progressions
in the middle which makes the song an uneven one. Incidentally it is
probably the first song that Harty wrote for Agnes Nicholls.

The year 1905 brought forth 'Three Traditional Ulster Airs', all
unsophisticated arrangements. 'The Blue Hills of Antrim' and 'Black
Sheela of the Silver Eye' are simple settings, and in between them
comes the much better known 'My Lagan Love', a haunting melody
with an imaginative harp-like accompaniment which contains the
first use by Harty of octave passages between the hands which
became a characteristic in later songs like 'Denny's Daughter', 'Hush
Song' and 'A Mayo Love Song'. 'Bonfires' has a good accompaniment to a less distinguished melody. Here again the opening phrase

---

1. 'Come, O come, my life's delight' (Campion), 'Now is the month of maying'
(anon.), 'Song of the Three Mariners' (anon.), 'Song of the Constant Lover' (Suck-
ling), 'Tell me not, sweet, I am unkind' (Lovelace).

(ex.22) makes it clear that Harty thought that the music was more important than just note and accent. 1905 also saw the publication of 'Sea-Wrack', though we know from his unpublished Memoir that he wrote it while still a boy at Hillsborough (see p.21). In it he has accurately caught the mood of Moira O'Neill's poem, and the music reeks of Ireland, of the sea, and of tragedy. Undoubtedly it is his most famous song, and has well survived countless performances at competitions; and when from time to time a festival throws up a non-plummy contralto with a talent for interpretation, its quality comes triumphantly across.

Ex.22   **Molto Allegro**

The 'Three Flower Songs' of 1906 are not Harty's most distinguished, though 'Gorse' has some light-hearted rhythm. A fourth song from the same year, 'The Ould Lad', has some warm and homely Irish philosophizing that no doubt was enhanced by Plunket Greene's intimate artistry.

The five settings of early poems have already been mentioned. They all have the qualities of their period rather than the personal stamp of Harty. 'Come, O come, my life's delight', 'The Song of the Constant Lover', and 'Tell me not, sweet' cannot really be said to match the poetry they set. A far more attractive song is 'Lane o' the Thrushes' (Cathal O'Byrne) which has a poised vocal line over an unusual accompaniment; colouring for phrases like 'swift brown stream' and 'shimmering shaft' is provided by an attractive scale-passage in the bass and far above it a chordal right hand.

The first three of the 'Six Songs of Ireland' (1908) are as good as anything Harty wrote. In 'Lookin' Back' the dark and sometimes forbidding colours of the Irish countryside are reflected in some ominous D minor music. 'Dreaming' shows the wistful, elusive

119

mood of the Irishman; and 'A Lullaby' is a fairy cradle song with a quite lovely melismatic refrain to each verse. 9/8 was one of Harty's favourite time signatures, and he uses it for the first and third of these songs; while the second is in 3/4 with many triplets, giving a similar metre. The other three songs in this set are perhaps less striking. 'Grace for Light' has a certain naive charm in the poem, but also an artificial element that does not sound quite sincere. 'Flame in the Skies of Sunset' (3/4 again with hints of 9/8) has some atmosphere, and 'At Sea' a bustling nautical flavour reminiscent of the 'Song of the Three Mariners'.

'Your hand in mine beloved', 'An Irish Love Song', and 'When Summer Comes' are typical of the ballads which were written in great quantities during the early years of the century. They by no means stand up to Harty's best. But the immediate pre-war years are dominated by the setting of Walt Whitman's poem 'By the bivouac's fitful flame' (1912) and the songs of 1913. The Whitman setting is one of Harty's best songs. He catches the mood immediately in a terse introduction, and holds it with dark textures and interesting harmonies, as well as some acutely-poised rhythmic values in the voice part. 'Across the Door' (1913) displays a keenly-felt contrast between the rowdy gaiety of the *céilí* and the strange quietness outside. Harty well expresses the intimacy of the coda at:

> The hawthorn bloom was by us
> Around us the breath of the South.
> White hawthorn strange in the night-time —
> His kiss on my mouth.

Herbert Hughes's song 'O Men from the Fields' is more familiar than Harty's setting 'A Cradle Song'. Both date from 1913 and it is unlikely that either composer heard the other's music before writing his own; yet they both have a similar modal quality. Harty, however, has some sixths in his accompaniment which recall not only 'Sea-Wrack' but also that un-modal composer Elgar.

I am inclined to think that 'A Drover' is the best song that Harty ever wrote. It has all his main qualities as a composer: virility, a personal Irish idiom, a good tune, a great variety of mood, and a finely-wrought accompaniment. The poem is enigmatic and the music reflects this in shifting harmonies and cross-rhythms (the time-signature is once again 9/8). 'The Rachray Man' is not far behind it. Here is that familiar character, the Irish woman complaining at her lot in having married the wrong man, and doing so with 'rueful humour' (Harty's direction) and mock resignation. There is something of the stage-Irish here, in the music as well as the words; but the exaggeration is appropriate and makes a great effect. The 9/8 time-signature is again tellingly used. In 'The Stranger's Grave' a young man lies buried in a graveyard dedicated to unbaptized babies, and he soliloquizes:

> O plotting brain, and restless heart of mine,
> What strange fate brought *you* to so strange a shrine?

The mood recalls a line in Tennyson's 'Maud': 'Why have they not buried me deep enough?'. Harty captures this morbid atmosphere with some ethereal music in an arioso style, and there is a passionate middle section. 'A Rann of Wandering' (1914) would be an ordinary song were it not for the momentum generated by a swift-moving triplet accompaniment. In 'The Wake Feast' Harty's sombre colours are again convincingly painted, this time to depict the young labourer's unfulfilled love for the daughter of the farm, now lying dead. Only the middle section in the major key is less effective.

After 1914 there is a long gap in the published songs until 1926, which saw four settings under the title 'Antrim and Donegal', two poems by Moira O'Neill and two by Elizabeth Shane. In the first song, 'The Two Houses', Harty tears immediately into his 'Children of Lir' or 'With the Wild Geese' mood with an orchestrally conceived accompaniment (yet another 3/4 song with triplets). The tempest is high, letting up only in the middle section as the singer dreams of 'gentle Ireland'. Harty's middle sections are not always his best music; they sometimes lack the imagination of his opening inspiration. But the stormy music returns and leads to a big climax and one of the very few long piano epilogues. 'The Little Son' has some subtle touches in the harmony, including an effective use of the flattened seventh. Both of the two Shane poems treat of the young married woman tied to the home. 'Hush Song' is an uncomplicated cradle song that complements the earlier 'Lullaby' and 'Cradle

121

Song'. 'Herrin's in the Bay' breezes along, but there is an underlying sadness of the girl who would rather be out with the fishermen: 'Sure I can sail a boat but what's the use of wishin'? When a girl is married she has other things to do'. And after the words 'Fillin' the bay where the stones are laid for wrack' Harty quotes from 'Sea-Wrack'. All these four songs have a compound time-signature except for the first which is 3/4 but noted throughout in triplets.

The 'Three Irish Folk Songs', with words by P. W. Joyce, were arranged in 1929. 'The Lowlands of Holland' is a similar tune to 'The Star of the County Down' and may well have a common ancestry. 'The Fairy King's Courtship' is pentatonic at times and at times Mixolydian, and 'The Game played in Erin-go-Bragh' is a rollicking tale of a good old Irish punch-up. In all three the strophic tunes are given variety with skilfully modified accompaniments.

Finally we come to the 'Five Irish Poems' of 1938. 'A Mayo Love Song', though original, looks back to the arrangement of 'My Lagan Love', with rhapsodical harp-like accompaniment. It is a big song with some extravagant and effective vocal declamation, as for example at the beginning (ex.23). Even here, though, notice the

Ex.23

curious word-rhythms in bars 6 and 8. 'At Easter' is a beautifully descriptive song with an organ-like accompaniment. 'The Sailor Man' is a typical Irish scherzo though it has an unusual ending for the voice alone. 'Denny's Daughter' has the poignancy of a man who has lost his young lover by death. 'The Fiddler of Dooney' matches 'The Sailor Man' in robustness, and makes us regret that Harty set no more of Yeats. The piano plays an important part in

Page from autograph of 'Ode to a Nightingale'

these last five songs, and in the first and fourth there is some prominent use of Harty's favourite device — the two hands in unison one or two octaves apart.

Of the two extended works, which lie somewhat apart from a discussion of the songs, 'Ode to a Nightingale' was written in 1907 for soprano or tenor and orchestra, and dedicated to Harty's wife. It is an expansive work, lasting more than twenty minutes, and it begins with a contemplative orchestral introduction, whose mood is retained by the singer during the first stanza. There is an interlude and a modulation from C to A flat before the next section: 'O for a draught of vintage'. Here the ecstatic mood is well caught by sweeping vocal lines and full-blooded orchestration (ex.24). For the sadness

Ex.24

and despair of the third stanza, the music becomes considerably slower and moves to F sharp minor. There is a momentary return to ecstasy at 'Away! Away! for I will fly to thee', but it soon leads to a Nocturne and a return to C major at 'Already with thee! tender is the night' (ex.25). The mood becomes more agitated, and there is a

Ex.25

huge climax, with the singer on top B, at 'pastoral eglantine'. This dramatic upsurge would probably not be foreseen during a reading of the poem, but it is convincing in performance. At 'Darkling I listen' the music repeats the singer's opening paragraph. It rises emotionally once more at 'Thou wast not born for death', only to sink back to rest in an echo of the orchestral introduction.

The melancholy beauty of Keats's poem is translated into music which has a coherence and an integrity in spite of being divided into many sections. It may be argued that the mood-changes in the poem are exaggerated in the music; but it would be almost impossible to set these words convincingly without magnifying their emotional content. Certainly Harty, with his sharp ear for orchestral colouring, could not be expected to do so. The work is most effective, and deserves more than an occasional hearing.

'The Mystic Trumpeter' was written in 1913 for the Leeds Music Festival, and is set for baritone solo, chorus and orchestra. Walt Whitman's kaleidoscopic pictures lend themselves to Harty's sectional treatment, and the music is enormously varied, with undoubtedly the most effective commentaries on the poem coming from the orchestra. The choral writing is too conventional to be really outstanding, and, as was remarked above in another context, Harty's personal characteristics are veiled behind a more general, turn-of-the-century style. The baritone has some good long sweeping phrases, especially in the setting of stanza 5.

Harty's songs, along with those of a dozen other composers of the first forty years of the century, have become victims of the changed emphasis in concert programmes. In the 1920s and 1930s, when the celebrity concert was in vogue, and when few Promenade Concerts did not include at least one if not two groups of songs in the second half, the successful song composer could be assured of a regular and deserved hearing. Now the fashion has changed, and even the giants of the 19th century, Schubert and Wolf and the rest, are not heard in the concert hall as often as they were.

What then of Harty's songs? It is to be feared that they will have to wait patiently for the fashion to turn again. Even if it does one cannot doubt that there are other songs almost equally neglected — those of Delius, Gurney and Warlock, for example — which will claim a higher place in the queue. But then, one hopes, 'A Drover', 'Lullaby', 'By the bivouac's fitful flame', and half a dozen others may take an occasional place on the concert platform. For there is no doubt that in his songs Harty, when he avoids the common utterance of some of his lesser contemporaries, has something original, striking and memorable to say.

IX CHAMBER MUSIC

Ivor Keys

Nearly all Harty's chamber music dates from early in his career, and indeed some of it was written in his teens at Hillsborough. Although there are some shorter pieces of individuality and charm, the main interest is the young man's absorption of the craft by trial and error, and by the practical experiences of a family string quartet — 'my mother and sister as violins, myself as viola (which I played very badly) and my father as cello'. These words come from the unpublished autobiographical Memoir of his years in the north of Ireland, and he has this to say of his composition at that stage:

> What with my church work, concerts of chamber music, organ recitals, orchestral concerts and accompaniment work, my life was fairly full, and any spare time was devoted to composition, principally songs and pieces for various instruments, though I also wrote three string quartets during this period. (Of these latter works I am not proud for they are naturally enough immature in style and unfinished in craftsmanship. On the other hand they do seem to me to show a certain lyrical freedom.)[1]

In considering the string chamber music first we need not flatly contradict the composer on immaturity, but we should remember that Brahms, the obvious exemplar in this field, was still composing music when Harty was a boy, and instead of harping on Harty's obvious derivations from Brahms we should rather admire the industry and native wit which enabled young Harty to achieve sufficient proximity to Brahms to provoke the comment in the first place. Three quartets indeed do survive, one of them — in A minor — in a manuscript dated 1898. It seems likely that the other two to which he refers were the op.1 in F and op.5 in A, which with three other chamber works won composition prizes in the Dublin Music Festival, the *Feis Ceoil*. He tells us in his Memoir that he entered more for 'the certainty of a good performance than the actual prize', a remark typical of a down-to-earth self-instructing attitude.[2]

1. Memoir, 7, 11.
2. Memoir, 18.

Chamber Music

We see from the front page of the manuscript that op.1 was composed by 'Herbert H. Harty'. We have not yet reached the dignity of 'Hamilton'. The immaturity resides mainly in the squareness of the rhythms and a difficulty over making logical and well-timed transitions from one key and section to another. But the outer fast movements have a compensating vivacity of subject-matter rather in Dvořák's manner. The Andantino Pastorale has a structural surprise: a hammered half-close (otherwise rather too big for the job) leads in, as a sandwich, a restatement of the main theme of the preceding Scherzo. In his enthusiasm towards the end of the work Harty seems to have in mind not solo strings but the orchestra which was to become his natural métier.

Neither of the Two Fantasiestücke (op.3) for piano trio has an individual title, but the first is an Andantino which reflects Schumann in the ardour and shapeliness of the tune. Interestingly the manuscript shows that Harty rightly cut eight bars of its reprise (after or before winning the prize?) even though they comprised an elegant rescoring. The alterations in the less individual second piece are interesting, making the string parts simpler but more individual, making a much more sophisticated gradation of the amount of motion in the piano part, and producing a Richard Straussian 'punch-line' out of the blue at the end.

The second String Quartet (in A, op.5) is now signed by 'H. Hamilton Harty' and represents, particularly in its first movement, a marked advance on op.1, being more incisive in instrumental detail and less square in its phrase-lengths. The opening gives a speedy sense of opening out, and again 'trial and error' leads to a cut of 16 bars either just before or just after the recapitulation (depending on how you look at it) which tautens the music. An abrupt modulation in the slow movement leads to an unmistakable reminiscence of the *idée fixe* of the Fantastic Symphony, and towards the end Berlioz again throws his shadow before us, when the viola and cello in octaves remind us of the Abruzzi Mountaineer's serenade from 'Harold in Italy'. (These details are the earliest evidence we have of his interest in the composer with whom — much later — his career as a conductor was to be so closely associated.) The heart-on-sleeve slow movement shows the composer at ease with his structure, whereas the

From the Autograph Book of the late Miss Nell Baguley

final movement, though lively in intent, has some uncertain dimensions caused by repetitions and some 'padding' — presumably what
Harty was alluding to in his own critique.

Under the pseudonym of 'Bessbrook' Harty won the Lewis-Hill
prize of fifty guineas in 1904 with the Piano Quintet in F (op.12),
which revels in the increased instrumental possibilities of the en-
larged medium. The orchestral musician emerges without having the
orchestral resources to deploy. This 'orchestral' effect is compounded
in the first movement by the strong rhythmic echoes of the main
motif of Tchaikovsky's Fourth Symphony, by some very Brahmsian
horn-calls, and by swirling string figuration which reads as though
Harty's imaginative ear heard the Hallé Orchestra in advance, rather
than a string quartet. But there is a markedly more adventurous
treatment of the key-scheme of the first movement. The elaborate
and indeed ornate second-subject paragraph in the exposition is begun and ended, not in the orthodox dominant, which would here be
C, but in the very unusual subdominant (B flat) — unusual because,
as students of tonal composition will know, the subdominant tends
to make an effect of home-coming, and at this point in the sonata-
form scheme one wishes to give the opposite effect. Harty drastically
limits this danger by swerving aside to B major in mid-course giving
himself thereby both a sudden feeling of widened horizons, which he
must have learnt from Brahms, and an opportunity for a striking
climactic modulation back to B flat. The reprise of the same material
in the recapitulation shows the same freedom, using three different
keys, none of them the orthodox one. Thus the composer, learning
by doing, is able to get more sense of movement over a long span of
music. There are still some alterations in the score, but they intro-
duce after-thoughts of piano figuration; only one is a structural cut.

The second movement is a 2/4 time scherzo-substitute whose main
tune, like the second subject of the first, begins by using the Irishism
of the pentatonic scale. In matters of detail we see the composer's
cool eye at work at some later stage: for instance, eight bars of rather
conventional arpeggios are marked 'out?' in his unmistakable hand.
But it would probably be wrong to suppose this conventionality was a
reason for possible removal (many years later Elgar was content with
equally ordinary, because effective, piano writing in *his* Piano Quin-

tet); a closer look shows that the arpeggios compete with an adequate clothing expressed better by the strings.

The slow movement and finale both show subsequent cuts, where Harty was clearly discontented, on reflection, with their shaping. The finale in particular gives the impression of lively first thoughts that perhaps the competition dead-line prevented him from deploying into a more effective structure. Nevertheless, there is in the work generally, and particularly in the detailed passion of the middle of the slow movement, enough to make one regret that it was to turn out to be his last substantial piece of chamber music.

A *Feis Ceoil* prize-work that was published (1903) heads the short list of cello pieces — Romance and Scherzo (op.8), dedicated to a cellist, W. H. Squire, whom we know from the Memoir to have been a frequent and friendly collaborator early in the century and who was to remain so for many years to come (see p.27). The basic ternary form of the Romance is preceded by an introduction which is touched by Wagnerian chromatics and which, after the movement's big climax, turns out to be more integral than it seemed. The Scherzo is less individual, its main theme being of the moto-perpetuo type associated with Popper. This said, it remains effective, and both pieces have an integrity of workmanship superior to the generality of the salon style. The second of the two cello pieces of 1907 (Der Schmetterling) is again in moto-perpetuo style, but the first (Waldesstille) shows a nice balance between length of piece and size of emotions, and between regular and irregular phrase-lengths, a respect in which the composer had obviously grown up since the quartets. Much later in his career (1928) he returned to this medium with a four-movement Suite, the finale of which he recorded with Squire in the same year.

On the title-page of the Fantasia for Two Pianofortes (op.6) Harty writes 'Conway: April 1902' and 'First Performance O'Sullivan's concert 17 April 1902'. This was a party-piece of no particular artistic pretensions, as the large number of pencilled cuts and other alterations confirms. The introduction, which recurs, has a number of Scottish Snaps in the rhythm (or perhaps one should say Celtic) and both the other main tunes begin with pentatonic outlines.

For piano solo there are two pieces, op.10, named 'Idyll' and

'Arlequin et Columbine', both dated 1904. 'Idyll' is a short 'Song without Words'; it is a salon piece but not without some sophistications, and affectionate and effective echoes of Chopin in the reprise. Columbine's share in the second piece is a waltz, but for all the Hyde Park address of the composer the Reeling gait of Arlequin cannot be disguised.

A 'Valse Caprice', in an undated manuscript, is of the same genre but requiring in places a more dexterous concert-style technique. On the other hand, another (undated) manuscript suite of 'Irish Fancies' shows a larger scope altogether, not only in its awareness of late-Romantic harmony, but also in continuity of construction and indeed in the technical demands of the piano writing. The individual numbers are: 'At Sea', a well-sustained combination of broad and *agitato* writing, 'The Stream in the Glen', which contains some delicate harmony, and 'The Spanish Stranger', a piece in 5/8 time with more than a few bravura moments. In fact this suite comprises the only piano pieces which show Harty as the thoroughly well-equipped pianist we know him to have been.

The three pieces for oboe of 1911 are not explicitly published as a suite. The repertoire is not so well-stocked that we should ignore these well-turned pieces, of which the 'Orientale' is the most enterprising in phrase-lengths and irregular rhythms. Two of the pieces were orchestrated by Harty, and two bars of the first ('À la campagne') were quoted by him on his bookplate, which shows a shepherd boy playing split-pipes.

Another piece which he later orchestrated is the Fantasy 'In Ireland' for flute and piano (1918; orchestral version, 1935). This has the programmatic heading 'In a Dublin street at dusk, two wandering street musicians are playing', and in the orchestral arrangement he is able to depict this musical dialogue more satisfactorily by including a solo part for harp as well as for flute. The Irish setting is much in evidence in the pentatonic turns of phrase, characteristic 'graces' and dance idioms. Formally, it is somewhat in the manner of a medley, beginning with a wistful 9/8 melody, followed by a dance-like Allegro moderato, and concluding (after a brief backward glance at the opening) with a Vivace which reworks the materials of the Allegro moderato in the style of a reel; and freed from any burdensome duty towards sonata design, Harty was here able to write one of his most elegant compositions, economical and well-proportioned.

Amongst the violin pieces are a suite of Handel movements which like the celebrated orchestral arrangements spring from a life-time's interest which began with Handel performances in his Hillsborough days: much later in life he orchestrated some of them (see p.107f). One other of the miscellaneous pieces deserves a mention as much for its biographical as for its musical interest: A Little Fantasy and Fugue for Carillon. This was written in 1934 as a result of an undertaking to the University of Sydney to compose a piece for the War Memorial Carillon there. It was first performed by a Miss Nettleship on Christmas Day 1934 and published by the University in 1935. For background I should like to quote from a speech made by Miss Olive Baguley when she unveiled the plaque at his birthplace at Hillsborough on 22 April 1964:

> The Bell Tower [of Hillsborough Church], where he told me that as a boy he longed to make music with those bells, seemed to hold a special fascination for him, and I believe that the Fantasy and Fugue which he wrote for the Carillon at Sydney University, following a tour of Australia, stemmed directly from that early ambition. A copy of the work is now in the Music Library at Queen's University, and I had the good fortune to one day hear him perform it himself on the famous Carillon at Loughborough.

Hillsborough again! The chamber music is a combination of prenticework and occasional pieces, and thus in a sense is unrepresentative, but it cannot fail to interest us as a documentation of a man finding himself, and combining intuition and industry in a mastery of characteristic instrumental sounds. But the threads of the ultimately cosmopolitan life all lead back to Ireland.

APPENDIX A:
DISCOGRAPHY

Cyril Ehrlich

The date in the left hand column refers to the review of the recording in *The Gramophone*, except when bracketed, in which case approximate dates of issue are given.

(i) AS CONDUCTOR

Bach, J. S.

March 1925	Concerto in D minor for two violins. A. Catterall and J. S. Bridge with orch.	Col L1613-15
June 1924	Suite no. 2 in B minor. R. Murchie (fl) and the Symphony Orch.	Col L1557-8

Balakirev, M.

Nov 1933	Russia. LPO.	Col DB1236-7

Bax, A.

Aug 1935	Overture to a Picaresque Comedy. LPO.	Col LX394

Beethoven, L. van

(Jan 1926)	Piano Concerto no. 3 in C minor. W. Murdoch and orch.	Col L1686-9
July 1927	Symphony no. 4 in B flat. Hallé.	Col L1875-9

Berlioz, H.

April 1935	Beatrice and Benedict, Overture.* LPO.	Col LX371
Oct 1932	Carnaval romain, Overture.* Hallé.	Col LX172
Feb 1935	Le Corsaire, Overture.* LPO.	Col DX664
June 1928	Damnation de Faust: Marche hongroise; Danse des sylphes. Hallé.	Col L2069
Dec 1935	King Lear, Overture. LSO.	Decca K792-3
Nov 1935	Marche funèbre (for the last scene of Hamlet).* LPO.	Col LX421

133

Discography

Jan 1934	Roméo et Juliette:	
	Part II: Roméo seul*; Tristesse; Concert et bal;	Col DB1230-1
Oct 1927	Grand fête chez Capulet.* LPO.	
	Queen Mab Scherzo. Hallé.	Col L1989
Dec 1935	Les Troyens:	
Nov 1931	March. LSO.	Decca K793
Aug 1971	Royal Hunt and Storm.* Hallé.	Col DX291
	Re-issue by World Record Club of works marked * above.	SH148

Brahms, J.

June 1925	Academic Festival Overture. Hallé.	Col L1637
Sept 1929	Hungarian Dance no. 5 in F sharp minor (transposed to G minor). Hallé.	Col 5466
Sept 1929	Hungarian Dance no. 6 in D flat (transposed to D major). Hallé.	Col 5466
(1929)	Violin Concerto. J. Szigeti and Hallé.	Col L2265-9

Bruch, M.

Dec 1925	Violin Concerto in G minor.	Col L1680-2

Clarke, J. (arr. H. Wood)

Sept 1927	Trumpet Voluntary. A. Harris, H. Dawber and Hallé.	Col L1986

Davies, H. W.

Sept 1927	Solemn Melody. C. Twelvetrees, H. Dawber and Hallé.	Col L1986

Debussy, C.

(pre 1925)	L'Aprés midi d'un faune (cut).	

Dvořák, A.

Feb 1928	Carnival, Overture. Hallé.	Col L2036
Feb 1924	Symphony no. 5 in E minor ('From the New World'). Hallé.	Col 9770-4 Col L1523-7

134

Discography

Elgar, E.

May 1927	The Apostles: Part II, By the Wayside. D. Labette, H. Williams, H. Eisdale, D. Noble, R. Easton, with Hallé chorus and orch.	Col L1968
Nov 1930	Cello Concerto. W. H. Squire and Hallé.	Col DX117-9
	Dream Children. Hallé.	Col DX325
March 1932	Enigma Variations. Hallé.	Col DX322-5

Flotow, F. von

Jan 1927	Martha: 'M'Appari'. C. Sherwood (T) and orch.	Col L1789

Handel, G. F., arr. Harty

Nov 1934	Concerto in D for Orchestra with Organ (Concerto 'B' in Händel-Gesellschaft Edition, ed. F. Chrysander, xlvii). H. Dawson and LSO.	Col LX341
June 1935	Royal Fireworks Music. LPO.	Col LX389-90
Dec 1935	Suite. LSO.	Decca K795-6
Nov 1933	Water Music, Suite. LPO.	Col DX538-9

Haydn, F. J.

Oct 1936	Symphony no. 95 in C minor. LSO.	Decca K798-9
May 1928	Symphony no. 101 in D major ('Clock'). Hallé.	Col 2088-91

Humperdinck, E.

Jan 1930	Hansel and Gretel: Dance Duet. Manchester School Children's Choir and Hallé.	Col 9909 Col SEG7705 Col SCD2092

Liszt, F.

June 1931	Hungarian Rhapsody no. 12 in C sharp minor (arr. as no. 2 in D minor). Hallé.	Col LX132

Mendelssohn, F.

May 1932	Symphony no. 4 in A ('Italian'). Hallé.	Col DX342-4

Discography

Mussorgsky, M.

Jan 1930	Khovanshchina: Prelude. Hallé.	Col 9908

Mozart, W. A.

March 1927	Bassoon Concerto, K191 (cadenza by Harty). A. Camden and Hallé.	Col L1824-6
Dec 1934	Divertimento in D, K334 (1st, 2nd, 3rd and 6th movements). LPO.	Col LX350-2
Sept 1933	Sinfonia Concertante, K364. A. Sammons, L. Tertis and LPO.	Col DX478-81
Nov 1926	Symphony no. 35 in D, K385. Hallé.	Col L1783-5
pre 1925	Violin Concerto in A, K219. A. Catterall and orch.	Col L1592-5

Purcell, H.

Jan 1930	Nymphs and Shepherds. Manchester School Children's Choir and Hallé.	Col 9909 Col SEG7705 Col SCD2092

Rimsky-Korsakov, N.

July 1929	Capriccio espagnol. Hallé.	Col 9716-7
	Flight of the Bumble Bee. Hallé.	Col 9908
April 1924	The Golden Cockerel: Introduction and Wedding March. Hallé.	Col L1533

Saint-Saëns, C.

March 1925	Carnival of the Animals. Symphony Orch.	Col L1617-9
Jan 1927	Cello Concerto no. 1 in A minor. W. H. Squire and Hallé.	Col L1800-2

Schubert, F.

Sept 1928	Alfonso and Estrella, Overture. Hallé.	Col L2122
April 1934	Marche militaire no. 1 in D (arr. Guiraud). LPO.	Col DX571
	Rosamunde, incidental music:	
Jan 1928	Overture. Hallé.	Col L1998
Sept 1928	Entracte 1. Hallé.	Col L2123
	Ballet, B minor. Hallé.	Col L2125
	Entracte 2. Hallé.	Col L2124
	Entracte 3. Hallé.	Col L2124
	Hirtenmelodie. Hallé.	Col L2124

136

Discography

	Ballet, G major. Hallé.	Col L2125
March 1930	Sonata in A minor, Arpeggione (arr. cello and orchestra, Cassadó). G. Cassadó and Symphony Orchestra.	Col LX1-3
May 1928	Symphony no. 9 in C. Hallé.	Col L2079-85

Senaille, J.B.

| March 1927 | Allegro spiritoso. A. Camden and Hallé. | Col L1826 |

Sibelius, J.

| April 1934 | Valse triste. LPO. | Col DX571 |

Smetana, B.

| Feb 1934 | The Bartered Bride, Overture. LPO. | Col DX562 |

Stanford, C. V.

| (pre 1925) | Shamus O'Brien, Overture. Hallé. | Col D1428 |

Strauss, R.

	Le Bourgeois gentilhomme:	
May 1924	Overture, Entrance and Dance of the Tailors.	Col L1552
	Minuet and Intermezzo.	Col L1555
July 1924	Dinner Music and Dance of the Young Cooks.	Col L1556

Tchaikovsky, P.

| June 1933 | Mazeppa: Cossack Dance. Hallé. | Col LX240 |
| | Piano Concerto no. 1. Solomon and Hallé. | Col LX19-22 |

Verdi, G.

| Jan 1927 | Rigoletto: 'Questa o quella'. C. Sherwood (T) and orch. | Col L1789 |

Wagner, R.

| March 1926 | Lohengrin: Act I, Prayer and Finale. M. Licette, M. | Col L1714 |

Discography

	Brunskill, F. Mullings, K. Lark, T. Bates, chorus and orch. (in English).	
May 1924	Parsifal: Good Friday Music. The Symphony Orchestra.	Col L1550-1
May 1924	Tristan's vision (from Act III 'Das Schiff' to 'wie schön bis du') without voice. The Symphony Orchestra.	Col L1551

Walton, W.

Jan 1936	Symphony no. 1. LSO.	Decca X108-13

Weber, C. M. von

May 1928	Abu Hassan, Overture. Hallé.	Col L2091

Weinberger, J.

May 1934	Schwanda the Bagpiper: Polka and Fugue. LSO.	Col LX293

(ii) AS PIANIST

Brahms, J.

(pre 1925)	Violin Sonata in D minor, op. 108: Adagio only. With D. Kennedy.	Col L1337
Feb 1925	Trio for clarinet, cello and piano, op. 114. With H. P. Draper and W. H. Squire.	Col L1609-11

Dvořák, A.

1931	Slavonic Dance no. 1. With Myra Hess.	Col DB1235

Grieg, E.

(c1923)	Violin Sonata in F, op. 8: excerpt, Allegro con brio and Allegro molto vivace. With D. Kennedy.	Col L1440
	Violin Sonata in G, op. 13: excerpt, Allegretto tranquillo and Allegro animato. With D. Kennedy.	Col L1440

Lambert, C.

March 1930	The Rio Grande. St. Michael's Singers, Harty (piano) and Hallé cond. Lambert.	Col L2373-4 (reissued by World Records, SH227, in 1976)

138

Discography

Mozart, W. A.

Dec 1923	Violin Sonata in A, K526. With A. Catterall.	Col L1494-6

Schubert, F.

(pre 1925)	Who is Sylvia. H. Eisdale (T).	Col D1419

Schumann, R.

(c1923)	Violin Sonata in A minor, op. 105: excerpts, Molto appassionata, Allegretto, Vivace.	Col L1338

(iii) AS COMPOSER

Instrumental

	Butterflies:	
Oct 1930	G. Cassadó	Col LB5
	B. Hambourg	HMV B3302
(Dec 1925)	W. H. Squire	Col DB1523
April 1927	Irish Fantasia. E. Kelly-Lange.	HMV B2419
	Irish Symphony. Scherzo only:	
Nov 1929	Hallé cond. Harty.	Col 9891
	New Concert Orch. cond. Leon.	Boosey & Hawkes 0 2194
	John Field Suite:	
July 1943	LPO cond. Sargent.	Col DX1118-20
Dec 1971	English Sinfonia cond. Dilkes.	EMI CSD3696
Nov 1929	Londonderry Air (arr. Harty). Hallé cond. Harty.	Col 9891
(1960)	Piano Concerto. L. Clark, orch. cond. Foggin.	Herald HSL106 (issued and reviewed but not listed)
Sept 1928	Scherzo (from Suite for cello and piano). W. H. Squire.	Col C2115
	Spring Fancies, for harp. S. Goossens.	HMV B1753
	With the Wild Geese:	
March 1927	Hallé cond. Harty.	Col L1822-3
Oct 1968	Scottish National SO cond. Gibson.	EMI ASD2400

Discography

Nov 1929	Bonfires. W. F. Watt (T).	Col 5574
	Colleen's Wedding Song. M. Phillips (S).	Parlophone E3630
	Cradle Song. J. McCormack (T).	American Victor 26705
July 1945	Lane o' the Thrushes. I. Baillie (S).	Col DB2178
	My Lagan Love:	
	A. Cox (T).	Parlophone E3555
	R. Hayward (T).	Decca F9084
	C. Lynch (T).	American Col 7637M
	G. Swarthout (Mez).	American Victor 16780
	Sea-Wrack. M. Brunskill (A).	Col 9687

See section (i) for arrangements of Handel

140

APPENDIX B:
HARTY'S WORKS

The date of composition (where known) is given *before* the name of the publisher; the date of publication is given *after* the publisher's name.

The letter 'Q' denotes that the composer's autograph is preserved in the library of The Queen's University, Belfast.

The final column gives page references in this book.

(i) ORCHESTRAL MUSIC

Title	Instrumentation	Date/Publisher	Auto-graph	Page
The Exile: Overture, op.2	2-2-2-2/4-2-3-1/ timp-perc/str	c1900:un-pub	Q	92-3,100
An Irish Symphony	3(3rd = pic)-2-eng hn-2-2/4-2-3-1/timp-perc-harp/str	1904, rev. 1915, 1924: Boosey, 1927	Q	28-9,37,74, 90-91,93-6, 100,139
A Comedy Overture	2(2nd = pic)-2(2nd = eng hn)-2-2/4-2-3-1/timp-perc/str	1906, rev. 1908: Schott, 1909; Universal, 1936	Q	29,90-91, 96-8
Violin Concerto in D minor	2(2nd = pic)-2(2nd = eng hn)-2-2/4-2-3/ timp-perc-harp/str	1908; Schott, 1909 (pf accomp't); C.E., 1920 (full score)		29,37,47, 80,86,90-91,98-9
With the Wild Geese: Poem for Orchestra	3(3rd = pic)-2-eng hn-2-b cl-2/4-2-3-1/ timp-perc-harp/str	1910: Novello, 1912		30,90,100-1,139
À la campagne, for oboe and orchestra (*see also under* Chamber Music)	solo ob+2-0-2-2/2 -0- 0/timp-perc-harp /str	Stainer & Bell, 1911 (pf accomp't); c1931 (orch.)	Q (2 copies of orch. score)	131

Title	Instrumentation	Date/Publisher	Auto-graph	Page
Orientale, for oboe and orchestra (*see also under* Chamber Music)	solo ob + pic-1-0-2-2/ 2-0-0/timp-perc-harp/str	Stainer & Bell, 1911 (pf accomp't); *c*1931 (orch.)	Q (2 copies of orch. score)	131
Proud Maisie: Incidental Music	1(= pic)-1 (= eng hn)-1-1/2-2-0/timp-perc-harp/str	1912: unpub	Q	91,102
Variations on a Dublin Air, for Violin and Orchestra (*also known as* Irish Variations for Violin and Orchestra)	2(2nd = pic)-2-2-2/2-2-0/ timp-perc/str	1912: unpub		30,90,101-2,106
The Singer of Shiraz: Incidental Music	2(2nd = pic)-1(= eng hn)-1-1/2-1-1/timp-perc-harp/str	1915: unpub	Q	75,91,102
Fantasy Scenes (from an Eastern Romance)	2(2nd = pic)-1-1-1/2-1-1/timp-perc-harp/str	1919: C.E. [1920]		37,90-91, 102-3
Suite for Orchestra (from the Water Music) (Handel arr. Harty)	2(2nd = pic)-2-2-2/4-2-0/timp/str	1920: Murdoch, 1922	Q	37,54,90-2, 103-4,135
Piano Concerto in B minor	2(2nd = pic)-2(2nd = eng hn)-2-2/4-2-3-1/ timp-perc/str	1922: C.E., [1923](orch. arr. for pf II)		30,37,90-1, 104-6,111, 139
Suite from the Music for the Royal Fireworks (Handel arr. Harty)	0-2-0-2/4-3-0/timp-perc/str	1923: Murdoch, 1924		37,54,90-2, 106-7,135
The Londonderry Air (arr. Harty)	solo vn-str-harp	Curwen, 1924		90,139
Polonaise, Arietta and Passacaglia (Handel arr. Harty)	3(3rd = pic)-2-2-2-dbn (optional)/2-3-0/ timp/str	Boosey & Hawkes, 1932	Q	107,135

Harty's Works

Title	Instrumentation	Date/Publisher	Auto-graph	Page
Concerto for Orchestra with Organ (Handel arr. Harty)	0-2-0-2/4-2-0/timp-org/str	Universal, 1934		107-8,135
In Ireland: Fantasy for flute, harp and orchestra (see also Chamber Music)	solo fl & harp + pic-0-1-eng hn-2-1/2-0-0/timp-perc/str	1915: Hawkes, 1918 (pf version); 1935 (orch.)	Q (orch. score)	90,131-2
Introduction and Rigaudon (Handel arr. Harty)	2(2nd = pic)-2-0-2/3-1-0/timp/str	Universal, 1935		108,135
The Children of Lir: Poem for Orchestra	3(3rd = pic)-2-eng hn-2-b cl-2-dbn/4-3-3-1/timp-perc-harp/str-S voice (concealed)	1938: Universal, 1939	Q; also sketch at Hillsborough Church	56-60,89-90,108-14
A John Field Suite (arr. Harty)	1(= pic)-1-1-1/1-1-0/timp-perc-harp/str	1939: Universal, 1939	Q	60,92 112-5,139

(ii) CHAMBER MUSIC

Title	Date/Publisher	Auto-graph	Page
String Quartet in A minor	1898: unpub	Q	126
String Quartet in F, op. 1	c1900: unpub	Q	26,126-7
2 Fantasiestücke for Piano, Violin and Cello, op. 3	c1901: unpub	Q	26,127
String Quartet in A, op. 5	c1902: unpub	Q	27-8,126-8
Fantasia for Two Pianos, op. 6	1902: unpub	Q	130
Romance and Scherzo for Cello and Piano, op. 8	Augener, 1903		27,130
Valse caprice: piano	c1904?: unpub	Q	131
Idyll; Arlequin et Columbine, op. 10: for piano	1904: unpub	Q	130-1

Harty's Works

Title	Date/Publisher	Auto-graph	Page
Irish Fancies for piano solo	c1904?: unpub	Q	131
Quintet in F, op. 12: pf, 2vns, va, vc	c1904: unpub	Q	28,129-30
Two Pieces for Cello and Piano Waldesstille—Wood Stillness Der Schmetterling—Butter-flies	Houghton, 1907; Forsyth, 1924		27,130,139
Suite for Violin with Piano (Handel arr. Harty): Rigaudon Arietta Hornpipe Passacaglia Polonaise Siciliano Allegro giocoso	Schott, 1910 (movements 1-4 only); 1920 (complete)		132
À la campagne: for Oboe and Piano (see also under Orchestral Music)	Stainer & Bell, 1911; orch. version c1931		131
Chansonette: for Oboe and Piano	Stainer & Bell, 1911	Q	131
Orientale: for Oboe and Piano (see also under Orchestral Music)	Stainer & Bell, 1911; orch. version c1931		131
Irish Fantasy, for Violin and Piano	Boosey, 1912		139
Spring Fancies: Two Preludes for Harp Solo	Novello, 1915		139
In Ireland: Fantasy for Flute and Piano (see also under Orchestral Music)	1915: Hawkes, 1918; orch. version 1935		90,131-2

Harty's Works

Title	Date/Publisher	Auto-graph	Page
Fanfare: 4 tpts and side drum	Fanfare no. 3, 1921, p.51		151
The Repose of the Holy Family (Berlioz arr. Harty): for Cello and Piano	c1928?: unpub	Q	
Suite for Violoncello and Piano: An Irish Prelude A Wistful Song Humoresque Scherzo-Fantasy	1928: Schott, 1928	Q	130,139
A Little Fantasy and Fugue for Carillon	1934: Univ. of Sydney, 1935		47,132
The Lasses of Donaghadee: Ulster Air arr. for piano	In *The Tree* (Ulster Soc. Prevention of Cruelty to Animals), Belfast, 1936, p.30		

(iii) VOCAL MUSIC

Unless stated otherwise all items are for solo voice and piano.

Title	Author	Date/Publisher	Auto-graph	Page
Across the Door	Padraic Colum	Novello, 1913		120
Antrim and Donegal:		1926: Boosey,	Q	121
The Two Houses	Moira O'Neill	1926		121
The Little Son	Moira O'Neill			121
Hush Song	Elizabeth Shane			118,121-2
Herrin's in the Bay	Elizabeth Shane			122
At Easter (*see* Five Irish Poems)				
At Sea (*see* Six Songs of Ireland)				

145

Title	Author	Date/Publisher	Auto-graph	Page
Black Sheela of the Silver Eye (*see* Three Traditional Ulster Airs)				
Blue Hills, The	John Arbuthnot	1906: unpub	Q	
Blue Hills of Antrim, The (*see* Three Traditional Ulster Airs)				
Bonfires	W.L. Bultitaft	1903: Boosey, 1903	Q	118-9,140
By the bivouac's fitful flame	Walt Whitman	Boosey, 1912		117,120,125
By the sea		1909: unpub	Q	
Carnlough Bay (Irish melody)		1921: unpub	Q	
Colleen's Wedding Song: 'I'm going to be married on Sunday'	P.W. Joyce	Boosey, 1905		140
Come, O come, my life's delight	Thomas Campion	Boosey, 1907	Q	118,119
Come up from the fields, father: ballad for chorus and orchestra	Walt Whitman	1912: unpub	Q (pf score)	117-8
Cradle Song	Padraic Colum	Novello, 1913		120,121,140
Denny's Daughter (*see* Five Irish Poems)				
Devon Maid, The	John Keats	1903: Augener, 1903	Q	117,118
Dreaming (*see* Six Songs of Ireland)				

Title	Author	Date/Publisher	Auto-graph	Page
Drover, A	Padraic Colum	Novello, 1913		120-121,125
Exile's Mother, An	Emily Lawless	1911: unpub	Q	
Fairy King's Courtship, The (*see* Three Irish Folksongs)				
Fiddler of Dooney, The (*see* Five Irish Poems)				
Five Irish Poems:		1938: Boosey	Q	56,86,122-4
A Mayo Love Song	Alice Milligan	1938		116,118,122
At Easter	Helen Lanyon			122
The Sailor Man	Moira O'Neill			122
Denny's Daughter	Moira O'Neill			118,122
The Fiddler of Dooney	W.B. Yeats			117,122
Flame in the Skies (*see* Six Songs of Ireland)				
Game played in Erin-go-Bragh, The (*see* Three Irish Folksongs)				
Gorse (*see* Three Flower Songs)				
Grace for Light (*see* Six Songs of Ireland)				
Heart of my Heart	Emily Lawless	unpub	Q	
Herrin's in the Bay (*see* Antrim and Donegal)				
Homeward	Harold Simpson	Novello, 1911		
Hush Song (*see* Antrim and Donegal)				
I heard a voice from heaven: for chorus (SATB) and organ		1901: unpub	Q	

Harty's Works

Title	Author	Date/Publisher	Auto-graph	Page
I'm going to be married on Sunday (*see* Colleen's Wedding Song)				
Irish Love Song, An	Katherine Tynan	Chappell, 1908		116-7,120
Lane o' the Thrushes	Cathal O'Byrne	1906: Boosey, 1907	Q	29,119,140
Little Song, The (*see* Antrim and Donegal)				
Lookin' Back (*see* Six Songs of Ireland)				
Lowlands of Holland, The (*see* Three Irish Folksongs)				
Lullaby (*see* Six Songs of Ireland)				
Mayo Love Song, A (*see* Five Irish Poems)				
Mignonette (*see* Three Flower Songs)				
My Lagan Love (*see* Three Traditional Ulster Airs)				
My Thoughts of You		1920: unpub	Q	
Mystic Trumpeter, The: for baritone solo, chorus and orchestra: 3(3rd = pic)-2-eng hn-2-2/4-3-3-1/timp-perc-harp-org(ad lib)/str	Walt Whitman	1913: Novello, 1913		31,117,125
Now is the month of maying	Anon., *c*1595	Boosey, 1907	Q	118

148

Title·	Author	Date/Publisher	Auto-graph	Page
Ode to a Nightingale, op. 16: for soprano (or tenor) and orchestra: 3(3rd = pic)-2-2-2/4-2-3-1/ timp-perc-harp/str	John Keats	1907: Breitkopf & Härtel, 1907 (pf score)	Q (pf score & full score)	29,64-6,98, 117,123-5
Ould Lad, The	Moira O'Neill	Boosey, 1906		119
Owl, The: partsong for SATB	Alfred, Lord Tennyson	unpub	Q	
Poppies (see Three Flower Songs)				
Rachray Man, The	Moira O'Neill	Novello, 1913	Q	121
Rann of Wandering, A	Padraic Colum	Novello, 1914		121
Rose Madness	W.L. Bultitaft	Augener, [1903]		117,118
Sailor Man, The (see Five Irish Poems)				
Scythe-Song	Riccardo Stephens	1910: Boosey, 1910	Q	
Sea Gipsy, The	Richard Hovey	Boosey, 1912		
Sea-Wrack	Moira O'Neill	c1895: Boosey, 1905	Q	20,29,119, 120,122,140
Six Songs of Ireland, op. 18:		1908: Boosey 1908	Q	29,119
Lookin' Back	Moira O'Neill			119
Dreaming	Cahir Healy			119
Lullaby	Cathal O'Byrne			120,121,125
Grace for Light	Moira O'Neill			120
Flame in the Skies	Lizzie Twigg			120
At Sea	Moira O'Neill			120
Song of Glen Dun, The	Moira O'Neill	Boosey, 1902		118

149

Title	Author	Date/Publisher	Auto-graph	Page
Song of the Constant Lover	Sir John Suckling	Boosey, 1909		118,119
Song of the Three Mariners	Anon., *c*1609	1907: Boosey, 1907	Q	118,120
Splendour Falls, The: partsong for SATB	Alfred, Lord Tennyson	Vincent Music, [1901]		
Stranger's Grave, The	Emily Lawless	Novello, 1913	Q	121
Tell me not, sweet, I am unkind	Richard Lovelace	Boosey, 1909		118,119
Three Flower Songs, op. 13:		Boosey, 1906		119
Poppies	L.B. Hay Shaw			117
Mignonette	L.B. Hay Shaw			117
Gorse	L.B. Hay Shaw			119
Three Irish Folksongs (arr):		OUP, 1929	Q	122
The Lowlands of Holland	P.W. Joyce			122
The Fairy King's Courtship	P.W. Joyce			122
The Game played in Erin-go-Bragh	P.W. Joyce			122
To the King: piano with organ obbligato	Riccardo Stephens	Chappell, 1911		
Three Traditional Ulster Airs (arr.):	Seosamh MacCathmhaoil	Boosey, 1905		29,118
The Blue Hills of Antrim				118
My Lagan Love				116,118,122, 140
Black Sheela of the Silver Eye				118
Two Houses, The (*see* Antrim and Donegal)				

Harty's Works

Title	Author	Date/Publisher	Auto-graph	Page
Wake Feast, The	Alice Milligan	Novello, 1914		121
When Summer Comes	Harold Simpson	J. Church, 1909		120
Your Hand in Mine, Beloved	Harold Simpson	Chappell, 1908		120

Harty also composed a Triple Chant in A, published in The Irish Chant Book, *formerly* Chants and Responses (*Association for Promoting Christian Knowledge, Dublin, 1907*).

Fanfare (see p.145). This very *à-la-mode* and short-lived periodical (October 1921-January 1922), edited by Henry Leigh, was the organ of the 'Fanfare Movement', whose purpose was to 'enfranchise the British musician among the other European artists'. There are articles by well-known figures such as Cocteau, Poulenc and Wellesz, drawings, and each issue contained a group of fanfares. Besides Harty, there are fanfares by Holbrooke, Poulenc, Satie, Prokofiev, Bliss, Bax, Auric, Vaughan Williams, Milhaud, Wellesz, Roussel, Havergal Brian, Malipiero and others. Harty was also among those who gave the magazine a send-off in its first issue. He wrote 'Good luck to *Fanfare*. It sounds interesting and — thank God — amusing. Best luck to the paper.'

151

DOCUMENTS

In addition to books and music from Harty's library, and manuscripts of many of his works, The Queen's University of Belfast possesses the following material (classified MS14):

1. An incomplete and unpublished autobiographical Memoir (autograph; see p.1).
2. Letters, telegrams, photographs and documents.
3. Scrapbooks (designated A,B,C,D,E) containing cuttings from newspapers and periodicals, letters, photographs, autographs, etc., compiled by Olive and Nell Baguley.
4. Lectures and articles by Harty (typescript unless otherwise stated):
   The Alsop Lectures (Liverpool University 1931-2). The Modern Orchestra:
      History and Growth of the Orchestra
      The Woodwind and Horns
      The Strings
      Conductors and Conducting
   The Approach to Berlioz (copied from *The Music Teacher*, September 1926)
   The Art of Pianoforte Accompaniment
   Beethoven's Orchestra: a Conductor's Reflections
   Berlioz (BBC broadcast, 2 March 1936)
   The Discouragement of English Music (28 August 1928)
   Modern Composers and Modern Composition
   Music in England (18 November 1935)
   On Listening to Music
   The Problem of Berlioz
   Some Problems of Modern Music (autograph)
   Variations on a Theme of Haydn: Brahms (16 February 1929)
5. Scripts of two BBC programmes about Harty: (a) Northern Ireland Home Service, 15 April 1946, with reminiscences by Nevin Foster, James Moore and Godfrey Brown; (b) London, 15 June 1951, with reminiscences by Lady Harty (Agnes Nicholls), W. H. Squire, Norman Allin, Clyde Twelvetrees, Alice Harty, Olive Baguley.

BIBLIOGRAPHY

Australian Broadcasting Commission: Programmes, 1934 Season

Barry, John. *Hillsborough: a Parish in the Ulster Plantation*. Belfast, 1962

Beecham, Sir Thomas. *A Mingled Chime*. London, 1944

C.— 'Hamilton Harty', *The Musical Times,* lxi (1920), 227-30

Cardus, Neville. *Autobiography*. London, 1947

— *Talking of Music*. London, 1957

Castellammare di Stabia. *Omaggio al musicista Michele Esposito* [1955]

Chicago Symphony Orchestra: Programmes, 43rd and 44th Seasons (1933-4, 1934-5)

Elkin, Robert. *Queen's Hall: 1893-1941*. London, [1944]

Fleischmann, Aloys (ed.). *Music in Ireland: a Symposium*. Cork, 1952

Foss, Hubert, and Goodwin, Noel. *London Symphony Orchestra*. London, 1954

Hallé Concerts Society: Programmes, 1920-34

Hamilton Harty Symphony Concerts: Programmes, 1929-30 and 1930-1 Seasons

Hollywood Bowl, 'Symphonies under the Stars': Programmes, 1931 Season

Kennedy, Michael. *The Hallé Tradition: a Century of Music*. Manchester, 1960

Pearton, Maurice. *The LSO at 70: a History of the Orchestra*. London, 1974

Rees, C. B. *100 Years of the Hallé*. London, 1957

Russell, John F. 'Hamilton Harty', *Music & Letters*. xxii (1941), 216-24

Scholes, Percy A. *The Mirror of Music, 1844-1944*. 2 vols, London, 1947

Shore, Bernard. *The Orchestra Speaks*. London, 1938

Szigeti, Joseph. *With Strings Attached: Reminiscences and Reflections*. London, 1949

THE CONTRIBUTORS TO THIS BOOK

JOHN BARRY is Rector of Hillsborough and Canon of the National Cathedral of St. Patrick, Dublin.

PHILIP CRANMER is Secretary to the Associated Board of the Royal Schools of Music. He was Professor of Music at Queen's University, 1954-70, and Manchester University, 1970-4.

CYRIL EHRLICH is Professor of Economic and Social History at Queen's University.

DAVID GREER is Hamilton Harty Professor of Music at Queen's University.

PHILIP HAMMOND is Head of Music at Cabin Hill School, Belfast, and part-time Tutor in Music at Queen's University.

LEONARD HIRSCH played in the Hallé Orchestra under Harty. In 1941 he was appointed leader of the newly-formed Philharmonia Orchestra. He was also leader of the Hirsch String Quartet and Musical Director of the BBC Training Orchestra (1966-9). He is now Chief Music Consultant for Hertfordshire and Professor at the Royal College of Music.

IVOR KEYS is Professor of Music at Birmingham University. He was Professor of Music at Queen's University, 1951-4 (Lecturer, 1947) and at Nottingham University (1954-68).

RAYMOND WARREN is Professor of Music at Bristol University. He was at Queen's University, 1955-72, as Lecturer (1955), Professor of Composition (1966) and Hamilton Harty Professor (1970).

INDEX

THE HALLÉ ORCHESTRA
A Rehearsal with Sir Hamilton Harty